AYAN CHALAN SIDDHANT

PRECESSION OF THE EQUINOXES

(AYANAMSHA AND SEASONAL CHANGE
RESEARCH CONFIRMED BY OTHER RESEARCH)

BIRENDER KUMAR NAUTIYAL

Translate by:-
NITIN SHARMA
SEEMA SHARMA

OUR LATE PARENTS

Mrs. Jamotri Devi Nautiyal

And

Mr. Jagdish Prasad Nautiyal

Contents

।। गणेश वंदना।।

खर्व स्थूलतनुम गजेन्द्रवदनम, लम्बोदरम सुन्दरम्।

प्रस्यन्दन्मदगन्धलुब्ध मधुप, व्यालोलगण्डस्थलं।।

दन्ताघातविदारितारिरूधिरैः, सिन्दूरशोभाकरं।

वन्दे शैलसुतासुतं गणपतिं, सिद्धिप्रदम कामदम्।।

वक्तुण्ड महाकाय कोटिसूर्य समप्रभं।
निर्विघ्नं कुरू मे देव सर्व कार्यषु सर्वदा।।

Book Reference

I start this book by bowing down at the feet of God. The reason for naming this book Ayan Chalan Siddhant is that the Sayan Sun is lagging behind the Nirayan Aries zero by a time scale of 20.41 minutes every year. He will again appear before Nirayan Aries zero after a certain period of 25771 years has passed. The target of the fixed period is to be completed by Ayan movement of 20.41 minutes every year, hence the book has been named Ayan Chalan Siddhant.

The starting point of Nirayan Aries is at an angular distance of 180 degrees from Chitra Nakshatra, this starting point of Aries is a fixed point. From the starting point of this fixed Aries we calculate the Spent ayanamsha of the planets in detail. On the basis of the planetary positions mentioned in our religious texts, it is believed that at the beginning of Satyayuga, the fixed and mutable Nirayan were together again at the starting point of Aries. Therefore, the main source of base calculation is the fixed point of Nirayan Aries.

In the beginning of the astrological civilization, our scholars and astronomers had expanded the calculations by considering the mentioned fixed point as the base, after some years they realized that our base point is not at its place, it has shifted towards the west from its place. This was called the lagging of the equinox or the movement of the equinox and the new point was called Char Bhachakra.

To understand the ayanamsha or seasonal change, you have to compare the third movement of the earth, which is called Ayana Gati in this book, with the annual movement of the earth. After the calculations, you will see that just as seasonal changes etc. occur under the annual movement, in the same way it also happens under the Ayan movement, the difference is only in years, that is, nature repeats its rules in micro and long form.

In the annual movement, the Sun starts moving from March 21, that is, the brightness increases and on June 21, it is slightly north of the east, again from June 21, the brightness decreases and the Sun appears to come back towards the east and on September 23, the Sun appears to move towards the east. It is exactly in the east direction.

In the same manner, it starts moving from 23rd September i.e. the brightness increases and on 22nd December it moves slightly south of the east, again from 22nd December the brightness decreases and the Sun appears to come back towards the east and on 21st March The sun is exactly in the east.

The above means that the Earth makes a complete revolution of 360 degrees around the Sun for its annual motion. In the middle of which the six seasons change, but it seems to us that the Sun goes a little north from the east and then again comes in the east direction and goes a little towards the south.

Similarly, Ayanamsha also makes a complete revolution of 360 degrees around the fixed star, during this period also six seasons change. The idea of seasons stated by the ancient masters in historical texts confirms the statement that the fixed star is moving towards the west.From zero degree till the completion of 90 degree ayanamsha, it moves slightly towards the north and after completion of 90 degree, it appears to come towards the east again for 180 degree ayanamsha.

Similarly, from 180 degrees till the completion of 270 degrees ayanamsha, it moves slightly towards the south and after completion of 270 degrees, it appears to come towards the east again for 360 degrees ayanamsha. In annual motion, the Earth revolves around the Sun and in Ayan motion, the Earth revolves around a fixed star. In the background of both of them, the starting point of Nirayan Aries is the base point of the calculations. Due to the above two movements, the six seasons keep rotating in front of this point.

Larger than calculations can be done easily with decimal calculations, hence decimal calculations are given in the first chapter of the book. How to convert Sign fractional to Sign decimal or Degree decimal is given in detail. Converting sign decimal to amount fraction minutes by reverse calculation has been explained. Apart from this, calculating year decimal, month decimal and their reverse and converting it back into year-month decimal has also been explained.

In the second chapter, how to calculate 25771 years of cycle, 71.59 years of one degree Ayanamsha, 70.56 years of one day of seasonal change, 50.29" Ayanamsha of one year, etc. have been explained in detail. Apart from this, it has also been explained in the same chapter that occurs in 'Ishtavarsha' and 'Ganavarsha' what difference.

In the third chapter, how many cycles passed from Satyayuga to the end of Dwaparayuga has been given in detail. The calculation of how many days of seasonal change or how much Ayanamsha had passed at the end of Dwapara Yuga has also been given in detail.

Vikrami Samvat, Shaka Samvat and AD started after how many years of Kaliyuga. On the day when Ayanamsha was again at the zero point, how many years of Vikrami Samvat, Shaka Samvat and AD had passed. The method of manufacturing Ayan Gati Chakra has also been explained in detail so that if you first build the device then it will be easier to take any kind of decision.

How can we use the same pattern of the Samvats that we currently use like Vikrami, Shaka and AD in any period? This is also given in simple language, because when calculated before any Samvat, there is a difference of seasonal change months, hence priority has been given to using the pattern. The Samvat Nirman is calculated from the Sun, the Sun is always there and will always be there, hence thought of the model.

Apart from this, in which Vikami, Shaka or AD pattern the end period of Dwapara Yuga or the beginning of Kali Yuga took place, its calculation along with the month and year entered is also given. The most enjoyable is the Kalisamvat decision chapter. The calculation of which date or which Vikrami Samvat month and in which entry the beginning of Kalinavasamvat should be considered at present has been given in detail.

The calculation of the dates on which Nirayan Sankranti was occurring or is occurring during the end of Dwaparayuga and in the present has also been given in detail. The method to bring about the beginning of Kaliyuga on 17/18 February BC is also given in this book. Apart from this, other researches have also been given to confirm the research on Ayanamsha and seasonal change.

Nirayan is constant and Sayan is variable, hence the angular distance from the zero of Nirayan Aries to the zero middle of Sayan Aries is called Ayanamsha. In the upcoming chapters, the calculations of Ayanamsha, seasonal change, solar month, entry, ahargana through Vaar, Date, Nirayan and Sayan Sun etc. are being given in detail, but before that it is necessary to briefly understand the method of decimal calculation.

The simplest methods have been given in the book, but one should not even try, that is, if someone has a habit of running away from mathematics, he cannot benefit in any way. keep in mind! The attainment of any subject matter can be achieved only through determination rather than education. Here I express my gratitude to my wife Mrs. Geeta Nautiyal, my younger brother Vinay Nautiyal and my younger brother-like astrologer friend Mr. Prashant Vats ji and bestow my blessings for their cooperation in correcting language errors. I am grateful to the following inspirational books that helped me in writing this book.

1. **Muhurta Chintamani**, Lecturer - Pt. Shri Kedardutt Joshi ji.
2. **Surya Siddhanta**, Lecturer – Prof. Shri Ramchandra Pandey.
3. **Aryabhatiya**, commented by Dr. Shri Satyadev Sharma.
4. **Grahalaghav**, Lecturer-Pt. Shri Ramswaroop Sharma.
5. **Nishansindhu**, Lecturer - Pandit Shri Jwala Prasad Mishra.
6. **Astronomy and Mathematics Astrology** Mr. Deepak Kapoor. The inspiration for research on Ayanamsha came from page 59 of the said book.

It is true that achieving perfection is never possible. Due to carelessness and lack of knowledge, I have expressed my curiosity in the middle of the book. If the scholars find my proposed language style harsh, I apologize and hope that in the near future, they will pave the way for improvement through their suggestions.

Chaitra Shukla Pratipada
27 Pravisthe Chaitra, 2080 Vikrami Samvat
9 April 2024 AD

Birender Nautiyal
Mobile : 8130235781

CHAPTER ONE

DECIMAL CALCULATIONS

Zodiac Sign Decimal:- Astrological calculations can be done quickly by converting the planetary positions into Zodiac Sign Decimal. First of all, by dividing the fractions by 60 and adding it to the fractions, the fraction decimal is obtained, by dividing the fractions decimal by 60 and adding it to the fractions, the fraction decimal is obtained, by dividing the fraction decimal by 30 and adding the amount, the fraction decimal is obtained.

The Planet are 5.25°45′50″, so
50 second/ 60=0.83+45minute=45.83 Minute Decimal,
45.83/60=0.7638+25 Degree=25.7638 Degree Decimal,
25.7638/30=0.85884+5 Sign =5.85884 Sign Decimal.

Reverse calculation formula:- Write the amount separately in decimal. The fraction is obtained by multiplying the digits after the decimal by 30. Where the previous amount was written separately, write down these fractions along with it, multiplying the digits after the decimal by 60 gives one decimal place. After writing the arts separately, the values are obtained by multiplying the digits after the decimal by 60. tians

Let 5.8588 zodiac sign decimal, except the last Zodiac Sign.
0.8588×30=25.7638 degree decimal,
0.7638×60=45.83 minute decimal,
Sold 0.83×60=50 second,
That is, 5.25°45'50" was obtained.

Year Decimal:- Adding minutes by dividing 60 in seconds, adding minutes in decimal and minutes in decimal, adding hours by dividing 60 in hours decimal and hours in decimal, adding days by dividing 24 in day decimal and division of fixed days of the month in day decimal. By adding month, month decimal is obtained and by dividing month decimal by 12 and adding year, year decimal is obtained. Suppose birth is on 14th July 1970 at 23 hours, 00 minutes and 10 seconds. The year 1970, July and 14th are not yet complete, hence one or two should be subtracted from them.

So 10/60=0.16667+00 min=00.16667 minutes decimal,
00.16667/60=0.00278+23hr=23.00278 hrs decimal,
23.00278/24=0.9584+13 days got=13.9584 days decimal,
13.9584/31=0.4502+6 month=6.4502 month decimal obtained,
6.4502/12=0.5375+1969 years=1969.5375 years decimal obtained.

Reverse calculation:- Let 1969.5375 years be decimal. 1969 is the last year, current year is 1970. calculation for balance,
0.5375×12=6.4502 months decimal, there are 6 full months, current month is July 1970, 0.4502×31=13.9584 days decimal, there are 13 full days, current month is July 14, 1970,
0.9584×24=23.00278 hours decimal,
0.00278×60=00.16667 minute decimal,
0.16667×60=10.0 seconds decimal received.

Note:- The numbers before the decimal confirm completeness and the numbers after the decimal indicate the current dynamics. As 23.34888 hours have been completed in decimal, the 24th hour is currently active. As 10.97287 days have been completed 10 days in decimal, the 11th day is currently dynamic. Like 5.8587 zodiac sign is 5 in decimal i.e. Leo zodiac sign has been completed, Virgo zodiac sign is currently dynamic. Understand the same in further calculations also.

Converting Sayan Sankranti date into month and year decimal: Sayan Sankranti dates will be required in further calculations, hence here we convert the Sankranti dates into month and year decimal. Month, month number, day and Sankranti date are given in the table below. Month decimals are obtained by subtracting one from the Sankranti date, dividing it by the number of days of the same month and adding the digits of the previous month. By dividing these month decimals by 12, the year decimal is obtained.

Table of the Sayan Sankranti days

Month	Sayan Sankranti	Total Days
January	20	31
February	19	28/29
March	21	31
April	20	30
May	21	31
June	21	30
July	23	31
August	23	31
September	23	30
October	23	31
November	22	30
December	22	31

Example:- 20 for January(-)1=19/31+0=0.61 January month decimal, 0.61/12=0.05 year decimal. For February 19(-)1=18/28+1=1.64 February month decimal, 1.64/12=0.14 year decimal. For March 21(-)1=20/31+2=2.65 March month decimal, 2.65/12=0.22 year decimal. By doing further calculations in the above manner, Sankranti date will be prepared as per the table given below.

Sayan Sankranti Month and Year Decimal Table

Mass	M.D.	Y.D.
January	0.61	0.05
February	1.64	0.14
March	2.65	0.22
April	3.63	0.30
May	4.65	0.39
June	5.67	0.47
July	6.71	0.56
August	7.71	0.64
September	8.73	0.73
October	9.71	0.81
Novembe	10.70	0.89
December	11.68	0.97

Note, the decimal places have utmost importance, here the whole decimal places are not given, it would be better if you do the calculations on microsoft excle sheet.

Hari Om

CHAPTER TWO

Decision on Calculation of Ayan Cycle Years

Subtract the days of Sayan year from the days of Nirayan year, the remaining Nirayan difference days obtained. By dividing these difference days into two separate parts into the days of Nirayan and Sayan year, the gross Years of the cycle including and without the days of seasonal change are obtained. There is a difference of one year between them, which is 365.256363 days of Nirayan year when the season changes.

In the gross years of Chakra, the digits after the decimal point indicate 12th April, hence by keeping the decimal of 21st March of the year in place of 12th April, the clear years of Ayan Chakra with and without seasonal change is obtained. If the decimal of 21st March of the year after the decimal is also removed from the Varshadi of Ayan Chakra along with the change of season, then it becomes Nirayan Chakra. The main basis for calculating Ayanamsha and seasonal changes are the years of Nirayan Chakra. Years of Ayana Chakra (with and without Season Change) has no special role in the calculation.

Chakra Calculations:- 365.256363(-)365.24219=0.014173 difference days ,
Days of Nirayan year 365.256363+0.014173=25771.28 including seasonal changes.
Days of Sayan year 365.24219+0.014173=25770.28 without seasonal change.

The difference between the Nirayan and Sayan years days of Ayan Chakra is obtained in the form of seasonal change year of 25771.28(-)25770.28=1 years. There is a seasonal change of 0.014173 (20.41 minutes) in the annual motion and a seasonal change of 365.256363 days in the 25771 years of the Ayana Chakra.

By including decimal 0.22 ((20/31+2)/12) in place of 0.28 in the year decimal season of Ayan Chakra, the exact 25771.22 solar years of Ayan Chakra are obtained. By removing the decimal of 21 March (0.22) years from the years of Ayan Chakra, the Nirayan Chakra of 25771 years is obtained, which is the basis of calculation.

Ayanamsh of one year:- By dividing 360 degrees of Bhachakamaan and dividing it by Nirayan Chakra, one gets the Ayanamsha of one year. By articulating 360 degrees of Bhachakamaan and dividing it by Chakra, the artistic Ayanamsha of one year is obtained. By dividing Chakra by 360 degrees of Bhachakamaan, the fractional Ayanamsha of one year is obtained.

Calculation:- (360×60×60)=1296000/25771=50.29" one year Ayanansha, (360×60)= 21600/25771=0.838' one year Ayanansha, 360/25771=0.014° one year Ayanansha.

Years of one degree:- By dividing Bhachakamaan in years of Chakra, the Years required to move one degree is obtained.

Calculation:- 25771/360=71.59 years, digits after decimal are 0.59×12=7.03 months, 0.03×(365.24219/12)=1.01 days, 0.01×24=0.35 hours, 0.35×60=20.97 minutes etc. The Sun takes 71 years, 7 months, 1 day, 0 hours and 20.97 minutes to move one degree of rotation.

Years of one day:- By dividing the days of Nirayan year by the years of the cycle, the time taken to walk one day is obtained, and by dividing the obtained years by 1440 minutes (24 hours), the seasonal change minutes of one year are obtained.

Calculation:- 25771/365.256363=70.56 years, 0.56×12=6.7 months, 0.7× (365.256363/12)= 20.43 days, 0.43×24=10.23 hours, 0.23×60=14.03 minutes etc. It takes 70 years, 6 months, 20 days, 10 hours and 14.03 minutes for one day's seasonal change. (24×60)=1440/70.56=20.41

minutes, Annually, 0.41×60=24.56 seconds, 0.56×60=33.63 per second etc., Annual Season Change consists of 20 minutes, 24 seconds and 33.63 per second.

Years of a Zodiac or Month:- By dividing the number of years of a cycle by 12, the years of a Zodiac or Month is obtained.

Calculation:- 25771/12=2147.58 years, 0.58×12=7.0 months. It takes 2147 years and 7 months to complete the twelfth part of Bhachakamaan.

Variance of constant variable:-
Including Ayan Chakra Season Change=25771.22
Ayan Chakra without Season Change= 25770.22
Nirayan Chakra=25771.00
1 degree ayanamsha years=71.59
1 day season change years=70.56
1 year ayanamsha=50.29"/0.83'/0.014°
years of the one zodiac sign or month=2147.58

Month total days:- The requirement of Nirayan month and Sayan month falls in the middle of Ayanamsh calculation, Vikrami for Nirayan month and Shaka Samvat month days for Sayan month are being given, for AD the calculation is done from the days of the respective month. Has been done, is, like January-31, February-28/29 etc. See table below:-

Month total days table.

ZODIAC	N.Month	T.Days	S.Month	T.Days	Month	T.Days
Aries	Baisakh	31	Chaitra	30/31	March	31
Taurus	Jyesth	32	Baisakh	31	April	30
Gemini	Ashadh	32	Jyesth	31	May	31
Cancer	Shravan	30	Ashadh	31	June	30
Leo	Bhadrapada	30	Shravan	31	July	31
Virgo	Ashwin	30	Bhadrapada	31	August	31
Libra	Karthik	30	Ashwin	30	September	30
scorpio	Margshirsha	30	Karthik	30	October	31
Sagittarius	Posh	30	Margshirsha	30	November	30
Capricorn	Magh	30	Posh	30	December	31
Aquarius	Phalgun	30	Magh	30	January	31
Pisces	Chaitra	30/31	Phalgun	30	February	28/29

Difference between Ishtavarsha and Ganavarsha:- In this calculation further calculation has to be done regarding Ishtavarsha and Ganavarsha, hence here the years from 1 January 2000 till present day is called Ishtavarsha and after subtracting Ayamsha zero year from Ishtavarsha, the remainder is called Ganavarsha. From the beginning of the first cycle till the completion of the 151st cycle, there was no Samvat in vogue from which Ganavarsha could be brought by subtracting the Ayanamsha zero year, just as further Ayanamsha zero year of AD has been brought by subtracting it. In such a situation only Ishtavarsha is considered as Ganavarsha. Therefore, the calculation from the beginning of Satyayuga till Ayanamsha zero years has been done considering Ishtavarsha as Ganavarsha. Due to this, there is no difference in the calculations of Ayanamsha and season change.

Hari Om

CHAPTER THREE

Zero Ayanamsha Year Ago Ayanamsha and Seasonal Change

In this chapter we are going to calculate Ayanamsha and seasonal changes. Ayanamsha is the angular movement from Nirayana Aries zero to Sayan Aries zero between and Season Change is the temporal motion of the fractional angle. Apart from this, due to the end of a cycle, era or end of the cycle, the offering and the offering gets divided into two parts, but the sum of the offering and the offering of the cycle is completed from 360 degrees of Ayanamsha and 365.256363 days of seasonal change.

Ganavarsha calculation method:- Kaliyuga is said to have 432000 solar years. Triyuga from Satya Yuga to Dwapar Yuga, for calculation, by multiplying the 432000 years of Kaliyuga once by four, once by three and once by two, the years of Satyayuga, Tretayuga and Dwaparayuga are obtained respectively. Sum these years from Satyayuga to Dwaparayuga and divide by the Varshadi of the cycle, the result obtained is the number of past cycles, that is, the said cycles have been completed between the total years of the three Yugas. To know the end of Triyuga, Ayanamsha, etc., by multiplying the digits after decimal (remainder) by Chakra, excluding the last rounds of the result obtained, (a) Ganvarsha etc. are obtained, (a) By subtracting Ganvarsha from Chakramaan, (b) Ganvarsha etc. are obtained.

Chakra Bhukta Percentage and Month Decimal: Multiply Kaliyugaman's 432000 by 9 and give the part of Chakra, the digit after the decimal in the obtained result is the Bhukta part of the current Chakra, multiplying this Bhukta part by 100, we will get Chakra Bhukta in percentage. It happens. By multiplying the percentage paid by 12, the decimal amount paid is obtained, the remaining calculation is as per the first method.

Ganavarsha calculation:- 432000×9=3888000/25771=150.87 gains in last round, 150 rounds were discarded, remaining 0.87 was adopted. 0.87×25771=22350 (a) Ganavarsha obtained, Chakramaan 25771(-)22350=3421 (b) Ganavarsha obtained. Keep in mind, A and B Ganavarsha are sayan solar years.

Ayanamsha calculation method: (a) Ayanamsha decimal is obtained by multiplying Ganavarsha by 360 and dividing it by Chakra Bhukta Chakra decimal is obtained by dividing the Ayanamsha decimal by 30 and then dividing it by 12. Multiplying Bhukta Chakra decimal by 12 gives Rashi decimal, Sayan Rashi decimal by multiplying the digits after the decimal by 30, Fraction decimal by multiplying the digits after the decimal by 60, minute decimal by multiplying the digits after the decimal by 60, minute decimal second decimal is obtained by multiplying the digits after the decimal by 60. P.second decimal is obtained by multiplying the digits after the decimal point by 60. This was the Bhukta Ayanamsha of the end of Triyuga or Dwaparayuga.

Ayanamsha calculation:- First place (a) Ganavarsha 22350×360/25771=312.21° Bhukta Ayanamsha obtained, 312.21°/30/12=0.87 Bhukta Chakra decimal, 0.87×12=10.41 Sayan Aquarius decimal, digits after decimal 0.41×30=12.21 degree Decimal, 0.21×60=12.68 Minute Decimal, 0.68×60=41.04 Second Decimal, 0.04×60=2.49 P.Second Decimal were obtained, during the end of Triyuga, the Sayan Sun was situated in 12 degrees, 12 Min., 41 Second and 2.49 P.Second of Aquarius. Was. In other words, at the end of Dwaparayuga, the 13th degree of Sayan Aquarius was moving in front of Nirayan Aries Zeropoint.

Chakra Spent Percentage and Monthly Decimal Calculations:- 432000×9=3888000/25771= 150.87 Receipt Past Chakra, Chakra was discarded, remaining 0.87 was adopted. 0.87×12=10.41 sayan aquarius decimal. Multiplying 0.87 by 100 gives the percentage of the present 151st cycle.

0.87×100=86.73 percent was obtained i.e. 86.73 percent of 360 degrees Ayanamsha had been completed. This calculation can also be done in another way, Total Ayanamsha 312.21°/30=10.41 Month/12=0.87 Chakra Bhukta Or got the offering of twelve zodiac signs.

Ganavarsha (b) Calculation method: At the time of the end of Triyuga, the 151st cycle was not completed. 0.87 Bhukta has been calculated under (a) Ganavarsha, the remaining
1-0.87= 0.13 Bhogya portion is calculated under (b) Ganavarsha.

Ganavarsha calculation:- Chakramaan 25771(-)22350 (a) Ganavarsha=3421 Ganavarsha (b) obtained.
Ascendant Calculations:- (b) Ganavarsha 3421×360/25771=47.79 degrees bhogya ascendant was obtained, 47.79°/30/12=0.13 bhogya chakra decimal, 0.13×12=1.59 Sayan Pisces (10.41+1.59=12 z.sign) decimal, decimal after of digit 0.59×30=17.79° decimals, 0.79×60=47.32' decimals, 0.32×60=18.96" decimals, 0.96×60=57.51'" decimals.

At the end of Ayanamsha Zerotime or 151st Chakra, Sayan Sun was situated in 0.13 percent of Bhogyansh of Chakra i.e. 17 Degree, 47 Minute, 18 Second and 57.51 P.Second. In other words, at the end of the 151st Chakra, the zero part of Sayan Aries was moving in front of Nirayan Aries Zero.

Chakra Bhogya Percentage and Month Decimal Calculation:- Chakra 151×25771= 3891421(-)3888000=3421/25771=0.13 Bhogya Quotient 151st Chakra, 0.13×12=1.59 Sayan Rashi Decimal. By multiplying 0.13 by 100, the benefit portion of the current 151st cycle is obtained in percentage. 0.13×100=13.27 percent was obtained i.e. 100 percent of 360 degrees ayanamsh (0.87 mukta + 0.13 bhogya) had been completed.

Seasonal change calculation method: (a) By multiplying Ganavarsha by the days of Nirayana year and dividing it by Chakra, the total number of days of seasonal change is obtained. By dividing the total number of days of seasonal change by the average of Nirayan month and dividing again by 12, the free part of the cycle or the consumed part of the year decimal is obtained. Multiplying this free cycle by 12, the month decimal is obtained.

In month decimal, day decimal is obtained by multiplying the digit after the decimal with Nirayan month average, hour decimal is obtained by multiplying the digit after the day decimal by 24, minute decimal is obtained by multiplying the digit after the hour decimal by 60. Second decimal is obtained by multiplying the digit after the minute decimal by 60. **These are the days of seasonal change of the present cycle at the end of Triyuga or Dwaparayuga.**

Season change calculation:- (a) Ganavarsha $22350 \times 365.256363/25771 = 316.77$ Total days of season change obtained, $316.77/(365.256363/12)/12 = 0.87$ Bhukta Chakra or Varsha decimal, $0.87 \times 12 = 10.41$ Phalguna month decimal, $0.41 \times (365256363/12) = 12.39$ days of seasonal change or 12.39 bhukta entries, $0.39 \times 24 = 9.35$ hours decimal, $0.35 \times 60 = 21.17$ minutes decimal, $0.17 \times 60 = 10.01$ seconds obtained. At the end of Triyuga, 10 months, 12 days, 9 hours 21 minutes and 10.01 seconds of seasonal change had occurred in 86.73 percent of the 151st Chakra.

Note, Nirayan is fixed, Sayan is variable, Nirayan Aries is in front of zero, the year starts from Baishakh solar month in the respective Sayan month (January etc.) in the part of Sayan zodiac that is present in that part.

The above 12.39 Bhukts are the Bhukt entries of seasonal change, Day etc. Narayan Sun, that is, the above mentioned entries have been spent in the annual and ayan cycle movements. By adding 12.39 days to the Sayan date falling in front of Nirayan Aries Shunya, clear Nirayan Sankranti date is obtained.

In the above manner, whatever Sayan Sankranti date will be falling in front of the Nirayan twelve zodiac signs.

By including the above Bhukta Dinadi, the dates of Nirayan Sankanti of twelve months are obtained, this is said in the context of annual movement. For Ayana Gati, the said offering has to be multiplied by

70.56 years and the auspicious years have to be added. This topic will understand in detail further:

Season change calculation:- (b) Ganavarsha 3421×365.256363/ 25771=48.49 total Bhogya days of season change received, 48.49/(365.256363/12)/12=0.13 Bhogya Chakra or year decimal, 0.13×12=1.59 month decimal, 0.59 ×(365.256363/12) Season change of 18.05 days, 0.05×24=1.16 hours decimal, 0.16×60=9.6 minutes decimal, 0.6×60=35.81 seconds were obtained. There was a seasonal change of 1 month, 18 days, 1 hour, 9 minutes and 35.81 seconds in the Ayanamsha Shunyakaal or the ending period of the 151st Chakra or 13.27[th] percent of the 151st Chakra.

Pushti:- At the end of a Chakra, sum the Ayanamsh etc. of both the parts of the Chakra (Bhakta and Bhogya), they should be as per their respective values. The sum of Ayanamsha of Part-1 and 2 should be 360 degrees Ayanamsha.

360 degrees Ayanamsha also means that at the end of 151st Chakra or 3421 years of Kaliyuga, Ayanamsha was zero degrees. Apart from this, also add the seasonal change days of Part-1 and 2, this sum should be 365.256363 days. The meaning of 365.256363 Days also means that at the end of 151st Chakra or 3421 years of Kaliyuga, the change in seasons was zero.

Confirmation of the Ayanasha of Part-1 and 2:- To confirm the calculation, we added the Ayanasha of the first part of the 151st Chakra (Triyuga End) and the Ayanasha of the second part (151Chakra Complate), 312.21°+47.79°=360° Ayanasha was obtained, hence the calculation is confirmed.

Confirmation of Seasons and Days of Part-1 and 2: To confirm the calculation, we added the season change days of the first part (Triyuga Sampati) and the second part (151st Chakra Complate) of the 151st Chakra, 316.77+48.49=365.256363 days were obtained, hence the calculation is confirmed.

Note, in the above Ayanamsha calculation, the sign of Sayan Aquarius has been mentioned, this means that the transition of Sayan Aquarius was going on in front of the zero point of Nirayan Aries or the starting point of Baishakh month. Ayanamsha is 312.21 degrees. If we divide this by 30, then Sayan Aquarius will be in front of the zero point of Nirayan Aries. Autumn is the season under Sayan Aquarius. Therefore, at the end of Dwaparyug, the year was starting from autumn season. Another example (c) Ayanamshaadi of Ganavarsha will be calculated further after determining the starting year of the Samvat (Era).

Bhukta Bhogya Table

	Spent	Yet to Pass	Total
Ganavarsha	22350.00	3421.00	25771.00
Ayanamsha	312.21°	47.79°	360°
season change	316.77 days	48.49 days	365.256363 days

Hari Om

CHAPTER FOUR

Samvat (Era) Decision

There is no Samvat in vogue from the beginning of Satyayuga till the present, hence Ayanamshaadi calculation from the end of Dwaparayuga till Ayanamsha Shunyakaal was done considering Ishtavarshas. But from the beginning of Kaliyuga, many Samvats had come into vogue between 3421 years of Ayanamsha, some of which are prevalent even in the present time, hence, only after proving them, Ayanamsha, season change etc. will be calculated by taking an example from the present.

Dwaparayuga ended in 22350 sayan solar years of the 151st Chakra. To get the beginning period of Kaliyuga, the seasonal changes up to the end of Dwaparayuga are included in 21st March and subtracted from the end period of Dwaparayuga and the remainder obtained is subtracted from its completed years. We have to find out the initial rainy days of Kaliyuga. Keep in mind, whatever number of years the Samvat started after Kaliyuga, it will have to be amended by subtracting its completed years according to its form.

Ayanamsh Shunyakaal Samvat Calculation:- In the above calculation, the Ayanamsh of Triyug end period was 312.21 degrees, 3421 sayan years were left for 360 degrees or Shunya Ansh Ayanamsh to occur. In the middle of these 3421 years, many eras like Vikrami Samvat, Shaka Samvat, AD etc. came into vogue. At present, Vikrami Samvat, Shaka Samvat and AD are in vogue, out of these, AD is being used the most, the thing worth noting is that complete calculations can be done only from Vikami (Nirayan) and Shaka (Sayan). But at present AD (Sankranti date) has become our necessity, whereas the angular and temporal motion of time cannot be read without either of Vikami (Nirayan) and Shaka (Sayan).

As in Ayanamsh Zerotime, how many years had passed since the beginning of the said Samvat, how much was Ayanamsh in that period? What was the Ayanamsha in the initial period of those eras? This has to be known.

Physically, Vikrami Samvat started after 3044 years of the end of Triyug, 57 years after the beginning of Vikrami Samvat (3044+57=3101 years), AD started, similarly 135 years after the start of Vikrami Samvat. After (3044+135=3179 years) or 78 years after the beginning of AD (3101+78=3179 years) the Shaka era is considered to be the beginning. Here you have also learned the importance of the main Shaka Samvat year 3179 used in the Tantra book Ahargan calculations.

If we add 3044 years to the current (31 December 2023 AD) Vikrami Samvat 2080, then 2080(+)3044=5124 Kalivarshas are obtained. If we add 3179 years to the current Shaka Samvat 1945, then 1945(+)3179=5124 Kalivarshas are obtained. If we include 3101 years in the current year 2023 AD, then 2023(+)3101=5124 Kalivarshas are obtained, here gross Kalivarshas are called, the exact Kalivarsha calculation will be done in some future chapter.

Broadly speaking, it can be said that Vikrami Samvat started after 3044 years of Kaliyuga, Shaka Samvat after 3179 years and AD 3101 years.

Note, the above mentioned distance of 135 years from Vikrami Samvat to Shaka and the distance of 57 years from Vikrami to AD is decreasing with time by time, this will be explained further in the calculation of Vikrami and Shaka Samvat.

Beginning of Kaliyuga before BC (reverse calculation):- In the calculations till now, we have found out the Ayanamsha and seasonal changes till Dwaparayuga. Now we will have to calculate the beginning period of Kaliyuga by doing the reverse calculation from the above mentioned era. To get the starting period of Kaliyuga from the 22350 sayan years, the end period of Dwaparayuga, 22350 will have to be subtracted from the complete years, 22350 (-)22350=0.00 years were obtained, if these were included in the above mentioned 3101 years of the initial period of AD, then only 3101 years were obtained.

By subtracting 3101 years from 3421 years, we get 3421-3101=320 years, i.e. after 3101 years of Kaliyuga initial period, AD started and till Ayanamsh Shunyakaal, 320 years of AD are obtained. had passed Decimalizing 21 March (0.22) years in 320 years (320 years+0.22= 320.22 sayan years), Ayanamsh zero year is obtained on 21 March 321 AD.

Dwaparyug end period istavharsh 22350+AD started year 3101+Ayanamsha Zerotime years 320=25771 total years of cycle.

Dwaparyug end period istavharsh 22350+Kaliyuga started 3421 year=25771 Total years of cycle.

Note, due to Samvat not being in vogue, Ayanamshaadi calculations were done by considering only the Ishtavarsha of 151st Chakra as Ganavarsha. Samvat came into vogue in the 152nd cycle, hence from the beginning of the 152nd cycle, calculations will be done including Sayan Sakranti dates to convert Ishtavarshas into Ganavarshas. Ishtavarsha (like 22nd December 2023 AD) are Sayan solar years, hence out of 320 years of Ayanamsh Shunyakaal, 21st March year has been made Sayan by including decimals in 320.22 years.

A.D.	
Ganvarsha (a)	22350.00
season change	-00000.00
end of sayan year dvaparayuga	**=22350.00**
Chakra	25771.00
End of sayan year dvaparayuga	-22350.00
Remaining ayanamsha zero year	**=3421.00**
Remaining ayanamsha zero year	3421.00
beginning of AD	-3101:00
Remain	=320.00
seasonal change	+(0.09+013)=0.22
Ayanushnyakaal A.D.	**=320.22**
Remain	320.00
beginning of AD	+3101.00
Remaining zero ayanamsha year end	=3421.00
sayan year dvaparayuga	+22350.00
Total years of Chakra	=25771.00

Beginning of Kali Yuga before Vikrami Samvat (Reverse calculation):- By subtracting the year decimal of the seasonal change that occurred during the end of Dwaparayuga from the 22350 sayan Varshadis, the starting period of Kaliyuga is obtained as Nirayan Varshadadi. Remember, Vikrami Samvat is inferior to seasonal changes, hence seasonal changes are being reduced. By including the remaining in 3044 years, the initial years of Vikrami Samvat from the beginning of Kaliyuga are obtained.

In the above calculation, the Chakra quotient was found to be 150.87, the digit after the decimal 0.87 (season change year decimal) was included in the decimal of 21st March year, 0.87+0.22=1.09 was obtained, this sum is more than one Chakramaan, hence it was divided by one Chakramaan. By subtracting 1.09-1=0.09 years decimals were obtained, on subtracting these from 22350 years, 22350-0.09=22349.91 Nirayan Varshadis and adding them to the 3044 years of the initial period of Vikram Samvat, 3044.09 Varshadis were obtained. This was a calculation of the seasonal change of 0.87 years till the end of Dwaparayuga to the decimal point.

Now I say the calculation from the end period of Dwaparyug or beginning of Kaliyuga till Ayanamsh Shunyakaal, 3044.09 years are subtracted from 3421.09 Varshadis (25771-25349.91) of Ayanamsha Shunyakaal, 3421.09-3044.09=377 years, Vikrami Samvat Varshadis till Ayanamsha Shunyakaal are obtained. It is said that Vikrami Samvat started after 3044.09 years of the initial period of Kaliyuga and 377 years of Vikrami Samvat had passed in Ayanamsh Shunyakaal.

For confirmation, 0.09 seasonal change year decimal was subtracted from 57 years, 57-0.09 =56.91 was obtained. If we include this in the above 3044.09 Varshadi, then we get the beginning period of Kaliyuga as 3044.09+56.91=3101.0 years, 3102 BC.

Dwaparyug end period istavharsh 22349.91+Vikrami started year 3044.09+Ayanamsha Zerotime years 377=25771 total years of cycle.

Dwaparyug end period istavharsh 22349.91+Kaliyuga started 3421.09 year=25771 Total years of cycle.

Vikrami Samvat	
Ganvarsha (a)	22350.00
March 21+season change	-0.09
Nirayan Surya End of Dwapara Yuga	=22349.91
Chakra	25771.00
Nirayan Surya End of Dwapara Yuga	-22349.91
Remaining ayanamsha zero year	=3421.09
Remaining ayanamsha zero year	3421.09
Start of the Vikrami Samvat	-3044.09
Ayanamsha Zero years	=377.00
Ayanamsha Zero years	377.00
Start of the Vikrami Samvat	+3044.09
Remaining ayanamsha zero year	=3421.09
Nirayan Surya End of Dwaparyug	+22349.91
Chakra Total Value	=25771.00

Beginning of Kali Yuga before Shaka Samvat (Reverse calculation):- Dwaparayuga From the 22350 years of the pre- subtract the decimal 0.22 (Bhukta 0.09 + Bhogya 0.13) from the year 22350 or add decimals to the year of change of season in the 22349.91 years of the above mentioned Vikrami Samvat, and then reduce it from its completed years to 3179. By combining it with Kaliyuga, the beginning period of Shaka Samvat is obtained.

22350 - 0.22 (21 March)=22349.78 Sayan Varshadi (annual) received, full year 22350(-) 22349.78=0.22+3179=3179.22 Varshadi, Kaliyuga started the said years before the beginning of Shaka Samvat period or Shaka Samvat started 3179.22 years after the beginning period of Kaliyuga. Had started.

Or
Seasonal change at the time of Dwaparanta month decimal 10.41 month/ 12=0.87 year decimal, 22349.91+0.87=22350.78 years, full year 22351(-)22350.78=0.22+3179=3179,22 years, beginning of Kaliyuga years before the initial period of Shaka Samvat. Or Shaka Samvat started after 3179.22 years of the beginning of Kaliyuga.

Subtracting these from 3421.22 years of Ayanamsh Shunyakaal, we get 3421.22(-)3179.22= 242 years, the years up to Ayanamsh Shunyakaal, that is, after the passage of 3179.22 years of the initial period of Kaliyuga,

Shaka Samvat started and 242 years of Shaka Samvat were spent in Ayanamsh Shunyakaal. Had finished.

For confirmation, by subtracting 0.22 (21 March year decimal) from 3179.22, the starting period of Kaliyuga was obtained as 3179.22(-)78.22=3101 BC.

Or by subtracting 135.13 years from 3179.22 Varshadi, the initial period of 3179.22(-)135.13 years=3044.09 Vikrami Samvat before Kaliyuga was obtained.

Dwaparyug end period istavharsh 22349.78+Shaka started year 3179.22+Ayanamsha Zerotime years 242=25771 total years of cycle.

Dwaparyug end period istavharsh 22349.78+Kaliyuga started 3421.22 year=25771 Total years of cycle.

Shaka samvat	
Ganvarsha (a)	22350.00
21 March decimal	-0.22
sayan sun end of Dwaperyuga	=22349.78
Chakra	25771.00
sayan sun end of Dwaperyuga	-22349.78
Remaining Ayanamsha zero year	=3421.22
Remaining Ayanamsha zero year	3421.22
shaka start year	-3179.22
Ayanamsha zero year	=242.00
Ayanamsha zero year	242.00
shaka start year	+3179.22
Ayan Zero Year+21 March	=3421.22
sayan sun end of Dwaperyuga	+22349.78
Ayan Chakra years	=25771.00

Note, Ayanamsha occurs in the zero period and Sayan Sun is at the initial zero degree of Aries, Vikrami Samvat Nirayan and Shaka Samvat are based on Sayan Sun. Therefore, how many years of these Samvattas had passed during Ayanamsha Shunyakaal? Let us calculate this. Apart from this, it should also be remembered that the initial period is always zero, like March 21 is included in Ayanamsha Shunyakaal 320.22, still it will be considered as zero, because if you include any date in the years of the Chakra, you will see the end of the Chakra. It will happen only on the date fixed by, remember that the cycle will always be of 25771 years of Nirayan, the reason is that the Sayan Sun has to revolve around Nirayan Aries Zero.

By adding 56.78 years to 320.22 for Vikrami Samvat, 377 elapsed years of Vikrami Samvat are obtained in Ayanamsh Shunyakaal. By subtracting 135 years from these years, 242 elapsed years of Shaka Samvat are obtained in Ayanamsh Shunyakaal.

320.22+56.78=377 years were obtained, 377 Vikrami Samvat years had passed in Ayanamsha Shunya period. Vikrami Samvat Varshadi 377-135=242 years, 242 Shaka Samvat years had passed in Ayanamsha Shunya period.

Ishtavarsha table.			
Samvatts pattern	A.D. Pattern	Vikrami Pattern	Shaka pattern
Dwaprant year	22350.00	22349.91	22349.78
Zero ayansh year	3421.00	3421.09	3421.22
Chakraman	25771	25771 0.91	25771
Annual status	0.00	0.91	078
Noun	Sayan	Nirayan	Sayan

Short:-

- Vikami Samvat Nirayan is the initial period of Sthira Bhachakra since it is based on the Sun. Whereas Shaka Samvat char is the initial period of Bhachakra. Nirayan Sun is without seasonal change and Sayan Sun is with seasonal change. Therefore, during Ayanamsha zero time, Vikrami and Shaka are zero after decimal.
- We can use the present pattern of Samvats like AD etc. in any era as we are doing today, hence the pattern has been written along with these Samvatts.
- The solar year keeps decreasing every year by a factor of 20.41 minutes due to seasonal changes, hence its duration is also short, due to which their statistical period increases.

- While Syan is the current Ayanamsha position. As at the end of Dwaparayuga, Ayanamsha was in Aquarius at a distance of 312.21 degrees from the fixed point, so this was its current position. From the zero point to the zero point again one solar year and from zero to the present Ayanamsha position is one solar year.

- Nirayan is a fixed point, from here the current position of Sayan is calculated or it can also be said that how much more time will it take for Sayan to reach Nirayan according to the annual and ayan motion?... It is measured by the angular method.

- Samvat determination calculation has been tabulated, see the above Samvat annual speed table, in Nirayan 22349.91 Ishtavarshaadi, 0.91 digits after the decimal point are Phalguna month or Aquarius sign under the annual speed. Whereas Sayan 22349.78 is Paush month or Capricorn under the annual speed of 0.78 digits after the decimal in Ishtavarshadi. The said Nirayan is said to be the symbol of Vikrami Samvat and Sayan is said to be the symbol of Shaka Samvat, because of the eternal existence of Nirayan and Sayan. In the AD model, 22350 solar years are also given in the table.

- In Ayanamsha Shunyakaal, there is a difference of zero days between Nirayan and Sayan or they are in the same entry, like when there is a change of season, there is a distance between them equal to the change of season and Dinadi. At the end of the cycle they are again located in the same entry.

Vikrami Samvat starting period Ayanamsh calculation:- Calculation for Vikrami Samvat (3044.09×360)+25771=42.52° Ayanamsh, from the beginning of Kaliyuga till the middle of Vikrami Samvat beginning period, 42.52 Ansh Ayanamsh had increased, if it is included in Dwaparant Ayanamsh then it would be 312.21(+)42.52=354.73 degrees Ayanamsha was obtained.

Season change in the beginning period of Vikrami Samvat:- Calculation for Vikrami Samvat (3044.09×365.256363)/25771=43.14 days, from the beginning of Kaliyuga till the middle of the beginning period of Vikrami Samvat, the season of 43.14 days had changed, this was included in the season change of the end period of Triyuga. So 316.77(+)43.14=359.91 days received Happened.

Ayanamsha calculation for the beginning of the year AD:- Calculation for the year AD (3101.0×360)/25771=43.32 degrees Ayanamsha, from the beginning of Kaliyuga till the middle of the beginning of AD, 43.32 degrees Ayanamsha had increased, if it is included in the Ayanamsha of the end of Triyuga then it would be 312.21(+)43.32=355.53 degrees of Ayanamsha was obtained.

Season change calculation from the beginning of AD:- Calculation for Vikrami Samvat (3101×365.256363)÷25771=43.95 days, from the beginning of Kaliyuga till the middle of the beginning of AD there was a season change of 43.95 days. If we include this in the seasonal changes of Triyuga end period, we get 316.77(+)43.95=360.72 days.

Shaka Samvat Start Time Ayanasha Calculation: Calculation for Shaka Samvat (3179.22×360)/25771=44.41 degrees Ayanamsha had increased by 44.41 degrees from the beginning of Kaliyuga to the middle of the beginning of the Shaka Samvat period. If this was added to the Ayanamsha of the end of Triyuga, then 312.21(+)44.41=356.62 degrees Ayanamsha was obtained.

Shaka Samvat Start Period Season Change Calculations:- Calculation for Shaka Samvat (3179.22×365.256363)÷25771=45.06 days, from the beginning of Kali Yuga to the middle of Shaka Samvat Start Period 45.06 days towards the change of season It was done, if it was included in the change of season of the end of Triyuga, then 316.77(+)45.06=361.83 days were obtained.

Vikrami Samvat Ayanamsh Shunyavarsha Ayanamsh Calculation:- Calculation for Vikrami Samvat (377×360)/25771=5.27° Ayanamsh, from the beginning of Vikrami till Ayanamsh Shunyakaal, 5.27 Ansh Ayanamsh had moved towards, if it is included in 354.73 Ansh Ayanamsh then it would be 354.73 (+) 5.27=360.00 degrees Ayanamsha obtained.

Vikrami Samvat Ayanasha Shunyavarsha Season Change:- Calculation for Vikrami Samvat (377×365.25)÷25771=5.34 days, the season change of 5.34 days from the beginning of Vikrami Samvat to Ayanasha zero period, added to 359.91 days is 359.91 (+) 5.34=365.26 days were received.

A.D. Ayanamsh Shunyavarsha Ayanamsha Calculation: Calculation for A.D. (320.22×360)/ 25771=4.47 Ansh Ayanamsh, from the beginning of Kaliyuga till 320.22 years of A.D. or Ayanamsh Shunyakaal, 4.47 Ansh Ayanamsh had become, if it is included in 355.53 Ansh Ayanamsh then it would be 355.53 (+) 4.47=360.00 degrees Ayanamsha obtained.

A.D. Solstice Zero Year Season Change Calculation: Calculation for A.D. (377×365.256363)/25771=4.54 days, from the beginning of A.D. till Ayanamsh Zero period there was a season change of 4.54 days, if it is included in 360.72 days then 360.72(+) 4.54= Received 365.26 days.

Shaka Samvat Ayanamsha Shunyavarsha Ayanamsha Calculation: Calculation for Shaka Samvat (242×360)/25771=3.38 degrees Ayanamsha, from the beginning of Kaliyuga, 242 years of Shaka Samvat or Ayanamsha till Shunyakaal had increased to 3.38 degrees Ayanamsha, it was included in 356.62 degrees Ayanamsha. So 356.62(+)3.38=360.00 degrees Ayanamsha was obtained.

Shaka Samvat Ayanasha Shunyavarsha Ritu change Calculation:- Calculation for Shaka Samvat (242×365.256363)/25771=3.43 days, from the beginning of Shaka to Ayanasha zero time, the season had changed by 3.43 days, if it is added to 361.83 days, 361.83(+) 3.43= 365.26 days were received.

Note, here the eras of Ayanamsh zero year have been determined, hence, in Ayanamsh zero year, there are 377 years of Vikrami Samvat and 242 years of Shaka Samvat, with zero after the decimal point, whereas in AD year, Vedhasiddha starts from 21st March. The said Samvat is the previous Samvat because the calculations are done on the basis of previous numbers only, hence in the Ayanamsh zero year, respectively, 1 Vaishakh 378th Vikrami Samvat, 21 March 321 AD and the present 1 Chaitra 243rd Shaka Samvat.

Hari Om

CHAPTER FIVE

AYANAMSHA AND CHANGE OF SEASON AFTER THE AYANAMSHA ZERO YEARS

We had already calculated the Ayanamshadi from the end of Dwaparayuga till Ayanamsha Shunyavarsha in the earlier chapters. After determining the Samvat etc., further calculations are being given in AD.

Ishtavarsha Decimal Calculation Method: For which ayanamsha etc. of the years is to be found, subtract one each from the year, month and days, then divide the days of the said month by adding the month to the month decimal, divide the month decimal by 12 to get the year. By combining, Ishtavarsha decimals are obtained. The method of making Rashi decimal and Year decimal has been given in detail in the previous chapter.

Ishtavarsha decimal calculation: By subtracting one from 22 December 2023, we get 21 days, 11 months and 2022 years received. Day 21/31+11 month=11.67 months decimal. Month decimal 11.67/12+year 2022=Ishtavarsha 2022.97 decimal obtained. Note: 21 days is divided by 31 days of December.

Ganavarsha calculation method: - By subtracting 320.22 from your favorite decimal, (c) Ganavarsha will be obtained. (c)Ganavarsha Like before, calculate according to the above Ayanamsha, season change calculation method.

Example Ganavarsha calculation:- 2022.97-320.22=1702.75 (c) Ganavarsha obtained.

Calculation of Spent Ayanamsha:- (c) Ganvarsha Decimal year 1702.75×360/25771=23.79° ayanamsha obtained, 23.79/30/12=0.07 bhukta chakra decimal, 0.07×12=0.79 Sayan Aries decimal, decimal later digits 0.79×30=23.79 Degree Decimals, Decimal Later Digits 0.79×60=47.16 Minute Decimals, Decimal Later Digits 0.16×60=9.87 Second Decimals, 0.87×60=52.44 P.Second Decimals were obtained, Sayan of Aries under 152nd Chakra in 22 December 2023 AD The Sun was situated in 0.07 per cent spent of the chakra namely 23ansha, 47kala, 9 vikala and 52.44 per vikala. In other words, in the said auspicious years of the 152nd Chakra, the 24th fraction of Sayan Aries was moving opposite Nirayana Aries Zero.

Chakra Bhukta Percentage and Rashi Decimal: Chakra 151×25771=3891421 year+1702.75 =3893123.75/25771=151.07 Bhukta Quotient, 0.07×12=0.79 Sayan Aries Decimal in 152nd Chakra. Multiplying 0.07 by 100 gives the percentage of the present 152nd cycle. 0.07×100=6.61 percent obtained i.e. 6.61 percent of the 360 Ayanamshas have been consumed or 6.61 percent of the 152nd Chakra has been freed.

Bhogya Ayanamsh:- Bhogya Chakra Decimal is obtained by subtracting the Bhukta Chakra Decimal from the Ayanamsh equivalent of Chakra by one. Convert the Bhogya Chakra Decimal into Sign, Degree etc. in the above manner.

Bhogya Ayansha Calculation: Ayanadi value of Chakra 1(-)0.07Bhukt=0.93Bhogya, Bhogya Chakra Decimal, 0.93×12=11.21 Sayan Pisces Bhogya Decimal, Decimal Later Digits 0.21×30=6.21 Ansha Decimal, 0.21×60=12.84Kala Decimal, 0.85×60=50.13 Vikala decimals, 0.13×60=7.56 pertivikala decimals were obtained, 0.93 percent of the 152nd chakra enjoyed as 6 Degrees, 12 Minute, 50 Second and 7.56 P.Second. In other words, at the end of the 152nd Chakra, the zero part of the Sayan Aries will be moving opposite the Nirayana Aries zero. Adding Bhukta to Bhogya gives the ending position of the 152nd chakra, Bhukta 0.79+11.21 Bhogyansha 12 zodiac.

Bhukta season change calculation: (c) Ganavarsha 1702.75×365.256363/25771=24.13 Total Bhukta days of season change obtained, 24.13/(365.256363/12)/12=0.07 Bhukta Chakra or Year Decimal, 0.07×12=0.79 Month Decimal, 0.79 ×(365.256363/12)=24.13 days' seasonal change, 0.13×24=3.20 hours decimal, 0.20×60=12.06 minutes decimal, 0.06×60=3.76 seconds were obtained. On December 22, 2023 AD, in the 152nd cycle, there was a seasonal change of 0 months, 24 days, 3 hrs. 12 minutes and 3.76 seconds.

Bhogya season change:- Bhogya chakra or year decimal is obtained by subtracting the seasonal value of chakra from one year. Bhogya chakra or year decimal is obtained. Convert the Bhogya chakra/year decimal into month, day etc. in the above manner.

Bhogya season change calculation: Value of Chakra or year 1-0.07Bhukta=0.93Bhogya year, 0.93×12=11.21 Bhogya month decimal, digits after decimal 0.21×(365.256363/12)=6.30 Days Bhogya season change, 0.30×24=7.31 hours decimal, 0.31×60=18.70 minutes decimal, 0.70×60=42.06 seconds were obtained. At the end of Ayanamsha Shunyakaal or the 152nd cycle, there will be a seasonal change of 11 months, 6 days, 7 hours, 18 minutes and 42.06 seconds in the 93.39th percent part of the Sayan Sun cycle.

Bhukta-Bhogya Table			
	Bhukta	Bhogya	Sum
Ganavarsha	1702.75	24068.25	25771.00
Ayanamsha	23.79°	336.21°	360°
Season change	24.13days	341.12 days	365.256363days

Note, by adding the bhukta of the above 23.13 days to 21st March or all the Sayan Sankranti dates, the dates of Dwadash (twelve) Nirayan Sankranti are known and by subtracting the bhukta from the average of Sayan month, the Bhogya would be obtained, the obtained Bhogya days would be included in the dates of Dwadash Nirayan Sankranti. By combining, the dates of Sayan Sankranti are obtained. Sayan Sankranti happens after Bhogya days. For example, if 6.3 days of Bhogya are added to the Sankranti date of Baishakh nirayan month, then Sayan Taurus Sankranti and summer season will start from 13.14+6.3=20 April, see Panchang for confirmation.

In the above Ganavarsha calculation, Ganavarsha has been obtained by subtracting 320.22 from Ishtavarsha. If Ganavarsha is to be derived from Vikrami or Shaka Samvat, then very small calculations have to be done, this has been explained well in the Shodhana year decimal calculation at the time of finding Vikami and Shaka Samvat.

- **Fraction Formula:** (Degree×365.256363/360)= Change of seasons, days, etc.
- **Year Formula:** (Years×365.256363/25771)=Change of seasons, days, etc.
- **Year Formula:** (Years/70.56)=Change of seasons, days, etc.

Brief:-

1. Nirayana is fixed and Sayan is variable, hence the variable point has to revolve around the fixed point.
2. A Nirayan Chakra is of 25771 years, if 21 March year is decimalised then it is called Ayan Chakra.
3. From zero ayanamsha on March 21 to 360 degree ayanamsha on March 21 are 25771 years.
4. March 21 has been included in the 3179 years of the initial period of Shaka Samvat or the quotient obtained by dividing 10.41 Bhukta month in decimal and Vikrami 10.95 month in decimal and dividing by 12, subtracting one year of Chakraman has been included in 3179 years. By adding Ayanamsha to Nirayana Surya, Sayan Surya is obtained, here consider the month decimal of Vikrami Samvat as Nirayana Surya, consider the change of season as Ayanamsha, sum of both of them has been done, if this sum is more than 12 then it has to be reduced from 12. Similarly, here it is reduced by one.
5. In the initial period of Vikrami Samvat, there are 3044.09 years, in the ending period of Dwaparyug, the Bhogya years of Nirayan Surya are i.e.

22349.91 years.

6. Vikrami Samvat Nirayan and Shaka Samvat are based on Sayan Sun. Nirayan Sun is without seasonal change and Sayan Sun is with seasonal change.

7. By adding Bhukta Days etc. to Sayan dates, Nirayan Sankranti dates are obtained and by adding Bhogya Days etc. to Nirayan Sankranti dates, Sayan Sankranti dates are obtained.

Hari Om

CHAPTER SIX

NIRAYAN ARIES SANKRANTI DATE, A ROUGH ESTIMATE

The main reason for finding out the benefits of seasonal change is that the Nirayana zodiac sign remains fixed but the Sayan zodiac sign is a visible moving zodiac sign, where is it at present? Or where was it in some era? How much seasonal change was taking place in that time? After knowing this, so that you do not get confused by the different conditions of Nirayana and Sayan, hence it was necessary to calculate the seasonal change Bhukta-Bhogya. The celestial sphere has been divided into twelve equal parts from Aries to Pisces. This is called Nirayana Rashi Chakra or Sthira Bhachakra. Each zodiac sign has its own-2 star clusters. The stars are distant, their speed is negligible compared to the Earth, they appear stable. Therefore, the angular distance from their straight line to the Earth is measured.

On the beginning day of Satyayuga, the Earth again started moving in line with the fixed star. After years, the Earth created a new rotation path in the clockwise direction or from east to west 20.41 minutes before coming in line with the star. Since that time, the Earth has been moving every year 20.41 minutes ahead of its previous path. Due to this, the seasonal cycle also keeps changing continuously. Due to the ongoing nature of this seasonal cycle, it is called Chara Bhachakra. Again, both fixed and variable particles are the same, but due to the uneven motion of the earth, they also become separate particles. The annual angular distance from the former path to the new path is 50.29". From the movement of the path, it appears that the Earth forms a flower petal in a clockwise direction every year from the line of the fixed star.

Because humans reside on the land, they are mobile along with the earth. Therefore, the variable wave appears to be stationary and the stationary wave appears to us to be moving in the anti-clockwise direction or from west to east. For this reason, depending on the different angular distances of the Earth from a fixed point over a while, the pole stars also appear to move from west to east.

The Earth's rotation path is moving clockwise relative to a fixed and fixed star. This is a movement in the middle of a long astronomical circle, the time value of this long circle is 25771 years. In other words, Ayanamsha takes 25771 years to move from the fixed star to the fixed star again. There is a seasonal change of 365.256363 days in the 360 degree Ayanamsh value of the elliptical Sayan Chakra. On this basis, season change of one day takes place in 70.56 years, season change of 10 days takes place in 705.5 years and season change of one month takes place in 2147.58 years (365.256363/12×70.56).

Due to slow motion, one season changes after 60 ion fractions (60×25771/360). When there is a difference of 120° ayanamshas, there is a change of two seasons. Money has been on this land not once but 151 times. At present there has been a seasonal change of 24.13 days. All this happens so slowly that it takes years, we will not survive, but for the generation of that time it will be a normal thing. In the middle of a cycle, each Vaishakhadi month gets its share of seasons. At present, seasonal changes similar to Ayanamsha should be known in detail.

At present (22 December 2023), there has been a seasonal change of 24.13 days in 1702.75 Ganavrasha. At the end of Triyug, there had been a seasonal change of 316.77 days, that is, the seasonal change was only 48.49 days behind the Nirayan Point and at present it is only 24.13 days ahead of the Nirayan Point, which means that in 72.62 S.C. (48.49+24.13) days, one More changes than the seasons have taken place in 5123.69 Kali years.

Aries Sankranti of Nirayan Sun currently occurs on 14th April (Baishakh) in the spring season, earlier it used to occur on 21st March in the spring season, the difference between the two has become 24.13 days. In this 444.83 years or Ishtavarsha 2022.97+444.83=2467.80 AD years (30.43-24.13×70.56-444.83 years) Aries Sankranti (Baishakhi) will be celebrated in the spring to summer season.

Seasonal change table				
	(a)Ganvarsh	(b)Ganavarsh	(c)Ganavarsh	(c)Ganavarsh
	316.77 bhukt	48.49 Bhogya	24.13 bhukt	341.13 Bhogya
Chakra	0.87	0.13	0.7	0.93
Month	10.41	1.59	0.79	11.21
Entries	12.39	18.05	24.13	6.30
Hours	9.35	1.16	3.15	7.37
Minutes	21.17	9.60	9.15	21.16

Table of the Sayan Sankranti days		
Sayan zodiac	Sayan Sankranti	Mass
Aquarius	20	January
Pisces	19	February
Aries	21	March
Taurus	20	April
Gemini	21	May
Cancer	21	June
Leo	23	July
Virgo	23	August
Libra	23	September
Scorpio	23	October
Sagittarius	22	November
Capricon	22	December

Example, Part-1:- The calculation of Gat Bhukta Bhogya Ayanamsh has been tabulated above. At the end of Triyuga or the beginning of Kaliyuga, the Sayan Sun was of Aquarius (10.41), known from Ayanamsha. Please note here, if Ayanamsha or change of season is to be taken in the month, then it will always be 21st March in decimal, if calculation is to be done from the entry. So that related January will be included in the month of Sayan Sankranti.

In the above Bhukta-Bhog table, if the entry 12.39 Bhukta in the third row of the first column is included in the related month 20th January, then to complete January, 11 days are required (31-20=11 days), subtract 11 days from 12.39 Bhukta (12.39-11=1.39 days), remaining 1.39 days or 2nd February (12.39+20=32.39-31=1.39) is obtained i.e. in the beginning of Kaliyuga, Nirayan Aries Sankranti used to occur on 2nd February. If 18.05 Bhogya entries are included in 2nd February, then (1.39+18.05=19.44) grossly, the end of Sayan Aquarius or the beginning of Sayan Pisces is obtained on 20th February.

It is known that what is known from the Bhukt and Bhogya entries, now I tell what is the significance of Bhogya month 1.59 month (48.49 days) in the above table, from any one fixed Nirayan Sankranti to its own fixed Sayan Sankranti middle of the said month. Or is it a day's distance. In the above example, Nirayan Aries Sankranti was happening on 2nd February, then Sayan Aries Sankranti would be on 22nd March (48.49 days away), how?... To complete 28 days of February, 26.61 days are required (28-1.39=26.61 days). , taking these days from 48.49 (48.49-26.61=21.87) the remaining days remained 21.87 days or 22 March. Similarly, other Sayan Sankrantis are also at a distance of 48.49 days from Nirayan Sankranti. Like the distance of seasonal change between Nirayan Taurus to Sayan Taurus will be 48.49 days, the distance between Nirayan Gemini to Syan Gemini will be 48.49 days. Similarly, understand further during the remaining Sankrantis also. Always keep this example in your memory.

Example, Part-3: Sayan Sun is of Aries, known from the ayanamsha of 22 December 2023 AD, Sayan Sun in Aries occurs on 21 March. In the above table, if we include the Bhukta entry 24.13 in the third row of the third column with March 21, then (20+24.13-31=13.14) is obtained as April 14, that is, in the year 2023 AD, Nirayan Aries Sankranti occurs on April 14. If 6.30 Bhogya entries are included on 14th April then (6.3+13.14=20.43) end of Sayan Aries or Sayan Taurus summer on 21st April. The beginning of the season was found in the context of the annual movement. If we say in the context of Sayan Chakra movement, then multiply 6.30 Bhogya entries by 70.56 years, then after 6.3×70.56=444.83 years, the position of Sayan Sun will remain in Taurus for the next 2147.58 years, in other words, it is Baisakhi or Nirayan Aries Sankranti. It will happen in the summer season. **See the calendar,** according to Vikrami Samvat, the month of Baishakh started on 14th April 2023 and the summer season started with the transition of the Sayan Sun to Taurus on the 7th entry of the month of Baishakh (6.3 Bhogya) or 20th April (6.3+13.14), The difference of one day may be due to the difference between the ayanamsha obtained from the above calculation and other ayanamshas.

Hari Om

CHAPTER SEVEN

MANUFACTURING METHOD OF AYAN CHAKRA YANTRA

After telling the method of above calculations, I consider it necessary to tell the method of manufacturing Sayan Chakra Yantra so that confusion does not Arise. Make a circle, keeping that circle in the middle, make a bigger circle one inch outside of it. Now mix the small and big circles and divide them into twelve equal parts and write them in the anti-clockwise direction from Aries to Pisces, then write the 27 constellations in their respective constellations, this is Sthira Bhachakra or Sthira Nakshatramandal.

The value of one zodiac sign is 30 degrees, hence, keeping a distance of 2 degrees, draw 15-15 lines between each zodiac sign and in the clockwise direction or from Aries to Pisces, considering Aries as 00 degrees, mark 2, 4 lines on each line. Write 6 degrees, remember, 30 degrees will be written on Pisces, by keeping writing at this interval of 2 degrees each, 90 degrees will be written on Capricorn, 180 degrees on Libra, 270 degrees on Cancer, 330 degrees on Taurus and again Aries. But 360 degrees will have to be written. Similarly, considering Aries as 00 degrees, write 13 degrees 20 minute at the end of Ashwini Nakshatra, 26 degrees 40 Minute at the end of Bharani, 10 degrees at the end of Krittika... etc.

Now Pisces and Aries between Chaitra, Aries and Taurus between Baishakh, Taurus and Gemini between Jyeshtha, Gemini and Cancer between Ashadh, Cancer and Leo between Shravan, Leo and Virgo between Bhadrapada, Virgo and Libra between Ashwin, Libra and Scorpio between Kartik, Scorpio And write Margashirsha between Sagittarius, Paush between Sagittarius and Capricorn, Magha between Capricorn and Aquarius and Phalgun between Aquarius and Pisces, this is called Nirayan Sthira Bhachakra. After that, the manufactured Chakra Yantra will become like the picture below.

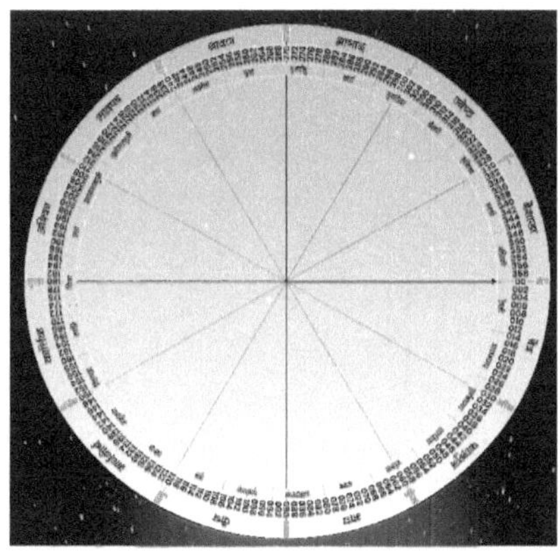

In the middle of the above picture, divide a small circle into twelve equal parts and write the zodiac signs from Aries to Pisces in the anti-clockwise direction. Aries 21st March, Taurus 20th April, Gemini 21st May, Cancer 21st June, Leo 23rd July, Virgo 23rd August, Libra 23rd September, Scorpio 23rd October, Sagittarius 22nd November, Capricorn 22nd December. Write 20th January for Aquarius and 19th February for Pisces.

On Aries line, 21st March along with Sayan month Chaitra, on Taurus 20th April along with Baishakh, on Gemini 21st May along with Jyeshtha, on Cancer 21st June along with Ashadha, on Leo 23rd July along with Shravan, on Virgo 23rd August. Bhadrapada with, Libra with 23rd September with Ashwin, Scorpio with 23rd October with Kartik, Sagittarius with 22nd November with Margarshish, Capricorn with 22nd December with Paush, Aquarius with 20th January with Magha and Pisces with 19th February. Write the same month of Phalgun.

Now Pisces and Aries and Aries and Taurus are in the middle of spring, Taurus and Gemini and Gemini and Cancer are in the middle of summer, Cancer and Leo and Leo and Virgo are in the middle of Monsoon, Virgo and Libra and Libra and Scorpio are in the middle of autumn, Scorpio and Sagittarius and Sagittarius and Capricorn are in the middle of pre-winter, write Winter between Capricorn and Aquarius and Aquarius and Pisces, this is called Sayan Char Bhachakra or Tropical Zodiac. After that, the manufactured Chakra Yantra will become like the picture below.

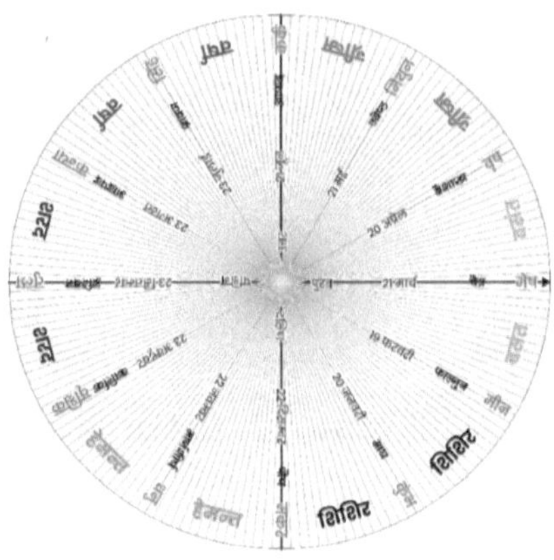

Cut the above Ayan Chakra into an equal circle and fix it by placing a nail right in the middle of the first Nirayan Bhachakra Yantra, so that the Ayan Yantra can rotate while remaining stable. See the Yantra picture below, it looks like this after placing the Ayan Yantra in the middle of the Nirayan Yantra. Keep in mind, Nirayan Aries and Sayan Aries remain on the same line during Zero Ayanamsha period.

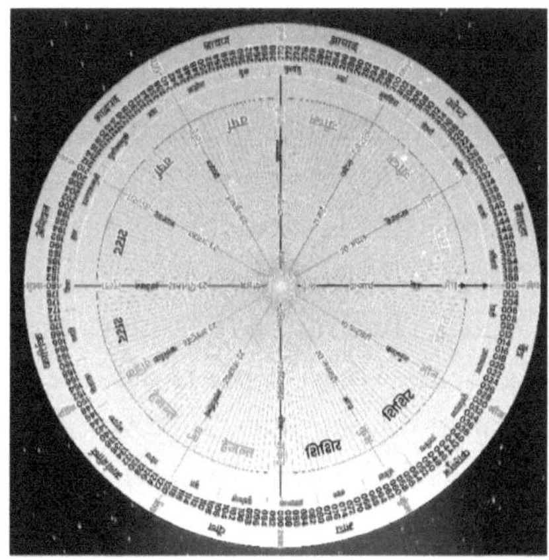

Estimate to fix Sayan Aries from the direct line of Nirayan Aries (Ayanamsh Zero Time) on Ayanamsh 23.79° (from Aries to Pisces) of current 22nd December 2023 AD, now the spring season of Sayan Aries will be in front of Nirayan Aries between 21st March to 20th April. The one is running away. Therefore, if March 21 is added to 24.13 days (current season change day), then physically we are getting Nirayan Aries Sankranti, the beginning of Baishakh month, on 13.14 (April 14).

Now let us have a look at the main Sankranti, the rainy season is falling in front of Nirayan Cancer Sankranti and from 21st June to 23rd July, hence around 15th July, Nirayan Cancer Sankranti is falling in front of Nirayan Libra Sankranti, autumn is falling and from 23rd September. The part of 23rd October is falling, hence Libra Sankranti is falling around 17th October, Winter in front of Nirayan Capricorn Sankranti and the part of 22nd December to 20th January is falling, hence Capricorn Sankranti is falling around 15th January.

Keep in mind, on 21st March during Ayanamsha Zero Time, both the Aries zodiac signs are together, if Ayanamsha increases then Sayan Aries (middle circle) moves forward in the clockwise direction at the same time as Ayanamsha. Behind Sayan Aries, other Sayan zodiac signs also move forward like Ayanamsha from their respective Nirayan signs. The more Ayanamsh increases, the more distance Sayan Rashi will remain from Nirayan Rashi, now the part of Sayan Bhachakra which will fall in front of

Nirayan Bhachakra, that part determines the date of season and Nirayan Meshadi ¼twelve sign.½ Sankranti.

The Ayanamsha of the end of Triyuga or the beginning of Kaliyuga period was 312.21, rotate the Sayan Aries sign of the Ayana Yantra by estimation and fix the Ayanamsha at 312.21. Now the winter part of Sayan Aquarius is falling in front of Nirayan Aries between 20th January to 19th February. Therefore, if March 21 is included in 316.77 days (seasonal change), then roughly the beginning of the year is being achieved from Nirayan Aries Sankranti, Vaishakh month on February 2. Now look at Nirayan Aquarius, from there Nirayan Aquarius Sankranti is being achieved in the Phalgun Nirayan month.

Keep in mind, whatever Sayan Rashi is in front of Nirayan Aries Zero, the Solar of the same Nirayan Rashi is in front of it. The same Nirayana Sankranti occurs in the month. For example, the present 22nd December 2023 AD is 23.79 degrees and Seasonal change is 24.13 days, Sayan Aries sign is in front of Nirayan Aries zero, hence Nirayan Aries. Sankranti is happening in the month of Baishakh. If the days of seasonal change are counted from the average days of Sayan month If subtracted, then after 30.43-24.13=6.30 days in annual motion, Sayan Taurus Sankranti, summer in Jyeshtha solar month. The season will begin.

Now let us have a look at the main Sankranti, the summer season is falling in front of Nirayan Cancer Sankranti and the period from 20th April to 21st May, hence around May, the rainy season is falling in front of Cancer Sankranti, Nirayan Libra Sankranti and from 23rd July to 23rd August. Therefore, Libra Sankranti was falling around 5th August, Pre-winter was falling before Nirayan Capricorn Sankranti and the part from 23rd October to 23rd November was falling, hence Capricorn Sankranti was falling around 9th November. The method of determining Sankranti by making an instrument has been explained in detail. It is hoped that after making the instrument, you will be able to remove the confusion arising from further calculations with the help of the instrument.

Note, in the above calculation, the Bhukta Degree etc. of Sayan Aquarius were determined, by multiplying these Degrees by 71.59 years, free Years are obtained, the Nirayan Surya also enjoys the season and period equivalent to these free Years. To not get confused, read the following explanation: The value of one zodiac sign under Ayana Chakra Gati is 2147.58 Varshadi. During Ayanamsha zero period, the transition of Sion and Nirayan Aries occurs at the same time, that is, both occur together at the first zero degree of Aries, after Ayanamsh is 30 degrees or after 2147.58 years, the transition of the mathematical variable Sion Sun to Taurus and the transition of Nirayan Sun to Aries are one. It happens in the same time period, that is, both of their two zodiac signs are in the same time period at the first zero degree, the Nirayan Sun will now come out of spring and will be called under the summer season.

After Ayanamsha is 60 degrees or after 4295.17 years, the mathematically variable Sayan Sun's Gemini transition and Nirayan Sun's Aries transition happen at the same time, that is, both of them occur at the same time at the first zero degree in their two zodiac signs. Similarly, further Sayan Rashi transition and Nirayan Sun's Aries transition always happen in zero degrees and at the same time period. In addition to the above mentioned motion, the Sun moves forward every year for the annual motion, as a result, 50.29" Bhogs continue to occur in that Rashi every year. After 2147.58 years, the Sun enters the next Sayan zodiac sign.

Nirayan Rashi remains fixed at one place in the month of Baishakhadi, in Ayanamsha Zerotime, Sayan and Nirayan are same, as Ayanamsh increases, Sayan Bhachakra gets separated from Nirayan Bhachakra and moves in the clockwise direction, due to this Nirayan is in the direction of Aries. In front of us are the signs of Aries, Sagittarius, seasons and their dates, but we feel that Nirayan Bhachakra is moving.

Hari Om

CHAPTER EIGHT

VIKRAMI, SHAKA SAMVAT BEFORE AND AFTER AND NIRAYANA AND SAYAN SUN

Vikrami and Kali Samvat are based on Sidereal Sun and Shaka Samvat are based on Tropical Sun. If you have found out the said Samvat, then it should be understood that you have also found out the approximate Rashi-Anshadi position of the Gross Nirayan and Sayan Sun. The main objective of this book was to present before you the research done on Ayanamsha and seasonal changes, but confirmation of Ayanamshadhi was also necessary, hence the research work continued further and other research results were obtained. The calculations after the ayanamsha and season change confirm the correct ayanamsha and season change in a rough way. In some future chapter, we will compare our Ayanamshadi with the Ayanamsha of other Ayanamshas by calculating the favorable and unfavorable results.

Vikrami and Shaka Samvat were not included under 151st Chakra, hence for the purpose of explaining here Nirayan Samvat is being addressed as Vikrami Samvat and Sayan as Shaka Samvat (straight calculation). Moreover Calculation is also being given from Vikrami and Shaka Samvat Purva (opposite) i.e. from Vikrami and Shaka Samvat. By counting backwards from the beginning period, the end period of Dwapara Yuga or the beginning period of Kali is calculated.being given.

After the above, the method of clarifying Vikami and Shaka Samvat in the present example. Will be called.

Refinement Year Decimal:- Make the month decimal by dividing the day of seasonal change by the average value of Nirayan month, similarly convert 21st March into month decimal and add both, if the sum is more than 12 then subtract 12 and divide by 12 to get the decimal. Year decimal is obtained.

Shodhan Year Calculation:- In the 151st Chakra, the seasonal change till Dwaparyug was 316.77 days and Ishtavarsha was 22350 years, on converting 316.77 days into month decimal, it is 10.41 month decimal and the month decimal of 21st March is 2.65. Seasonal change month 10.41+2.65 (21 March)=13.05 month decimal obtained, it is more than 12 months, hence this sum was subtracted from 12 months, 13.05-12=1.05 month decimal remained, dividing it by 12 made year decimal, 1.05/12=0.09 Refinement year decimals obtained.

Note, whatever seasonal change we get in Ayan Chakra is included in 21st March, in other words, by counting the days of seasonal change from 21st March, we get to know Nirayan Sankranti. From the Ayan Chakra obtained from the above Ayan Chakra construction method, you will see Nirayan month Jyeshtha from the Bhukta part of Dwaparayug example, but this will be wrong, because Sayan Chakra moves in the clockwise direction, which is also the opposite direction to the Nirayan solar months. To know the actual month, the calculation of the above month Dashamalav 10.41 (11th Phalgun month) should be started from Vaishakh.

Total days of the month						
Zodiac	N.Month	T.Days	S.Month	T.Days	Month	T.Days
Aries	Baisakh	31	Chaitra	30/31	March	31
Taurus	Jyestha	32	Baisakh	31	April	30
Gemini	Ashadh	32	Jyestha	31	May	31
Cancer	Shravan	30	Ashadh	31	June	30
Leo	Bhadrapada	30	Shravan	31	July	31
Virgo	Ashwin	30	Bhadrapada	31	August	31
Libra	Krtaik	30	Ashwin	30	September	30
Scorpio	Margashirsha	30	Kartik	30	October	31
Sagittarius	Posh	30	Margashirsha	30	November	30
Capricon	Magh	30	Posh	30	December	31
Aquarius	Falgun	30	Magh	30	January	31
Pisces	Chaitra	30/31	Falgun	30	February	29/29

Nirayan Samvat (Vikrami Pattern) Direct calculation method: By subtracting Shodhan year decimal from Ishtavarsha, the annual speed of Nirayan Sun is obtained in year decimal. In year decimal, month decimals are obtained by multiplying the post-decimal digit by 12, entry decimals are obtained by multiplying the post-decimal digit by the days of the respective month, reduced decimals are obtained by multiplying the post-decimal digit by 60. The decimals are obtained by multiplying the digit after the decimal by 60.

Calculation:- Dwaparyug Ishtavarsha 22350(-)0.09=22349.91 Nirayana Samvat year decimal was obtained. Decimal digits after decimal in year decimal 0.91×12=10.95 Phalguna month decimal, 0.95×30=28.43 entry decimal, 0.43×60=26.03 ghati decimal, 0.03×60=1.54 pal decimal obtained. In the annual movement, at the end of Dwaparyug, the Nirayan Sun was situated on 29th entry, 26th Ghati and 1.54 Pal Decimal of Phalgun month.

Note that every year, Kalisamvat new year started on 29th entry of Phalgun Nirayana month, that is, Kaliyuga started on 29th entry of Phalgun month, because Nirayan is stable. Therefore, the new year of Kalisamvat will always be celebrated in the said month only, whereas this is not possible in AD. The date changes every 70.56 years in AD. The calculation of Kalisamvat in AD is given in a later chapter.

Nirayan Surya Vidhi:- Consider the above Nirayan Samvat month decimal as Rashi decimal, multiplying the digit after the decimal by 30 gives degrees decimal, multiplying the digit after the decimal by 60 gives minute decimal, number after decimal is obtained. Second decimals are obtained by multiplying the digits by 60.

Calculation:- 10.95 Rashi (Aquarius) decimal, 0.95×30=28.43° decimal, 0.43×60=26.03' decimal, 0.03×60=1.54" decimal were obtained. In the annual movement, at the end of Dwaparayuga, the Nirayana Sun was situated in 28 degrees, 26 Minute and 1.54 Second Decimal of Aquarius.

Sayan Samvat (Shaka counterpart) Direct calculation method: Nirayana Samvat 0.87 years in decimal year (S.C.Bhukta) By adding decimals and subtracting one, Sayan Samvat year decimals are obtained. year in decimal after decimal By multiplying the digit after the decimal by 12, month decimals are obtained, by multiplying the digit after the decimal by the days of the respective month, we get reduced decimals, by multiplying the digit after the decimal by 60, we get reduced decimals, Multiplying the latter digit by 60 gives the second decimal place. Note, the annual motion position of the Nirayana Sun is 0.91 years in decimal, when it is decimalized by 0.87 years then it becomes more than one, hence one is being asked to subtract.

Calculations: Nirayana Samvat Year Decimal 22349.91+0.87-1=22349.78 Sayan Samvat Year Decimal Obtained Happened. The digits after the decimal in the year decimal were 0.78×12=9.35 Paush month decimal, 0.35×30=10.65 entry decimal, 0.65×60=38.71 ghati decimal, 0.71×60=42.58 pal decimal. In the annual movement, at the end of Dwaparyug, the Sayan Sun was situated at 11 Pravistha, 38 Ghati and 42.58 Pal Decimal of Paush month. Note, the difference between Nirayan month decimal 10.95 and Sayan month decimal 9.35 is 10.95-9.35=1.59 Bhogya season change month decimal, it shows the balance of season change.

Sayan Surya Method:- Sayan Surya is obtained by adding Ayanamsh 10.41 Rashi decimal to the above mentioned Nirayan 10.95 Rashi decimal, if this sum is more than 12 then subtract 12. Or consider the above Sayan Samvat month decimal as Rashi decimal, by multiplying the digit after the decimal by 30, we get degree decimal, by multiplying the digit after the decimal by 60, we get minute decimal, by multiplying the digit after the decimal with 60. we get second decimals are obtained.

Calculation:- 10.95+10.41=21.35-12=9.35Rashi (Capricorn) decimal, digits after decimal 0.35×30=10.65 degree decimal, 0.65×60=38.71 minute decimal, 0.71×60=42.58 second decimal obtained. In annual motion, at the end of Dwaparayuga, the Sayan Sun was situated in 10 degrees, 38 minute and 42.58 second Decimal of Capricorn. See the table below, Shishir Ritu and Uttarayan are known from the position of Sayan Sun in Capricorn.

Vikrami Samvat before, opposite calculation method: The end of Dwaparyug and the beginning of Kaliyug had started 3044.09 years before the beginning of Vikrami Samvat, see the chapter regarding 3044.09 years in determining the beginning period of Samvat.

In year decimal, post decimal digits were 0.09×12=1.05 Jyeshtha month decimal, 0.05×30=1.67 entry decimal, 0.67×60=40.24 ghati decimal, 0.24×60=14.36 pal decimal were obtained. According to Vikrami pre-calculation, at the end of Dwaparayuga or the beginning of Kali, 2 entries of Jyeshtha month, 40 Ghati and 14.36 Pal decimal were obtained. Note, if the Bhukta of the basis is known then the remainder of the basis is always Bhogya, like in the direct calculation of the above mentioned Nirayan Samvat, Phalgun month (10.95) was obtained by counting from Baishakh month, now it is obtained by subtracting 10.95 from the 12 months of the year. By counting the remaining results from Baishakh, Jyeshtha month will be obtained, 12-10.95=1.05 (2), Baishakh 1, Jyeshtha 2. Also note the entries, 28.43+1.67=30 total days of Phalgun month.

Confirmation:- By adding 3044.09 to the annual speed of Sun 22349.91 Bhukta years, it was 22349.09+3044.09=25394 years, to this the elapsed years of Ayanamsha Shunyakaal were added, 25394+377=25771 years, the value of Chakra was obtained.

Nirayan Samvat Ishtavarsha 22349.91+3044.09 Vikrami before
A total of 25394 years before the beginning of Vikrami Samvat.

Suppose a person has been asked to calculate till November, if a person calculates directly from January to November, then he will get 11 months, if someone else calculates reversely from December to November, then he will get 2 months, both are true. The above reverse calculation has been stated in the same manner. It would be appropriate if the months obtained by reverse calculation are reduced by 12.

Sayan Sankanti, Season and Month Table				
Month	Season	Ayan	Sayan Rashi	S.Sankranti
January	Winter	Uttra	Aquarius	20
February	Spring	Uttra	Pisces	19
March	Spring	Uttra	Aries	21
April	Summer	Uttra	Taurus	20
May	Summer	Uttra	Gemini	21
June	Monsoon	Dakshina	Cancer	21
July	Monsoon	Dakshina	Leo	23
August	Autumn	Dakshina	Virgo	23
September	Autumn	Dakshina	Libra	23
October	Pre-Winter	Dakshina	Scorpio	23
November	Pre-Winter	Dakshina	Sagittarius	22
December	Winter	Uttra	Capricon	22

Pre-Shaka Samvat, opposite calculation method:- The end of Dwapara Yuga and the beginning of Kaliyuga started 3179.22 years before the beginning of Shaka Samvat, see the previous chapter regarding 3179.22 years in determining the beginning period of Samvat. Decimals after decimal in year decimal were 0.22×12=2.65 Jyeshtha month decimal (counting from Chaitra), 0.65×30=20.65 entered decimal, 0.65×60=38.71 ghati decimal, 0.71×60=42.58 pal decimal were obtained. According to the pre-calculation of Shaka Samvat, at the end of Dwaparyug or the beginning of Kali, there will be 21 entry, 38 Ghati and 42.58 pal of Jyeshtha month. In the direct calculation of the above Sayan Samvat, Paush month (9.35) was obtained by counting from Chaitra, now by subtracting 2.65 from the 12 months of the year, Jyeshtha month will be obtained by counting from Chaitra, 12-9.35=2.65 or 3, then Chaitra 1, Baishakh 2, Jyeshtha 3.

Confirmation:- Annual speed of Sayan Sun is 22349.78. By adding 3179.22 in Bhukta years, it is 22349.78+3179.22=25529 years, in this the elapsed years of Ayanamsha Shunyakaal are added, 25529+242=25771 years, the value of Chakra is obtained.

Sayan Samvat Year 22349.78+3179.22 shaka before
Total 25529 years before Shaka Samvat initial period

Samvat Varshadi Table.				
	Nirayana	Before Vikrami	Sayan	Before Shaka
Year	22349.91	3044.09	22349.78	3179.22
Month	10.95	1.05	9.35	2.65
Entries	28.43	1.67	10.65	20.65
Ghati	26.03	40.24	38.71	38.71
Pal	1.54	14.36	42.58	42.58

The above calculation was from the beginning of Kaliyuga till Ayanamsha Shunyavarsha i.e. the calculation was done before Ayanamsha Shunyavarsha, now the calculation after Ayanamsha Shunyavarsha is being given below.

Refinement Year Decimal:- Make the month decimal by dividing the day of seasonal change by the average value of Nirayan month, similarly convert 21st March into month decimal and add both, if the sum is more than 12 then subtract 12 and divide by 12 to get the decimal. Year decimal is obtained.

Calculation of purification year:- Season change till 22 December 2023 AD in 152nd cycle is 24.13 days and Ishtavarsha. It was 2022.97 years old, converting it into month decimal gives 0.79 month (0.07 year) decimal and The month decimal of March 21 is 2.65. Seasonal change month 0.79+2.65 (21 March) = 3.44 month decimal was obtained, dividing it by 12 to make year decimal, 3.44/12=0.29 refinement year decimal was obtained.

Current Vikrami Samvat:- By subtracting Shodhana year decimal from Ishtavarsha, the annual speed of Nirayana Sun is obtained in year decimal. These years include 57 years, then by multiplying the digit after the decimal in the year decimal by 12, month decimals are obtained, by multiplying the digit after the decimal with the days of the respective month, the entry decimals are obtained, Lowering decimals are obtained by multiplying the first digit by 60, multiplying the digit after the decimal by 60 gives third decimals.

Calculations: Desired Year 2022.97-0.29+57 Year=2079.69 Vikrami Samvat Year Decimal was obtained. In the year decimal, the decimal after digits 0.69×12=8.24 Paush month decimal, 0.24×30=7.18 Pravishte decimal, 0.18×60=10.9 Ghati decimal, 0.9×60=54.13 Pal decimal were obtained. In annual motion, Nirayan Sun was at 8 Pravishtha, 10 Ghati and 54.13 Pal Dashamala of Paush month in Vikmi Samvat 2080 (22 December 2023).

Current Nirayan Sun:- Nirayan Samvat Month Decimal should also be understood as Rashi Decimal, by multiplying the digit after the decimal by 30, degree decimal is obtained, by multiplying the digit after the decimal by 60, we get minute decimal, the digit after the decimal is obtained second decimals are obtained by multiplying by 60.

Calculation:- 8.24 Rashi (Sagittarius) Decimal, digits after decimal 0.24×30=7.18Ansh Decimal, digits after decimal 0.18×60=10.90 Kala Decimal, 0.90×60=54.13 Vikala Decimal obtained. In annual motion, Nirayan Sun was situated in 7 degrees, 10 minute and 54.13 second decimal of Sagittarius.

Current Shaka Samvat:- Shaka Samvat year decimal is obtained by subtracting 135 from the Vikrami Samvat year decimal by adding 0.07 year (R.P.Bhukta) decimal. In year decimal, month decimals are obtained by multiplying the post-decimal digit by 12, entry decimals are obtained by multiplying the post-decimal digit by the days of the respective month, reduced decimals are obtained by multiplying the post-decimal digit by 60. The decimals are obtained by multiplying the digit after the decimal by 60. Note, the annual speed of Nirayana Sun is 0.69 years in decimal, when 0.07 years of seasonal change is added to it, then the Sion speed is known.

Calculation:- Vikrami Samvat year decimal 2079.69+0.07-135=1944.75 Shaka Samvat year decimal was obtained. The digits after the decimal in year decimal were 0.75×12=9.03 paush month decimal, 0.03×30=0.97 entry decimal, 0.97×60=58.06 ghati decimal, 0.06×60=3.87 pal decimal. In annual motion, on 22 December 2023, the Sayan Sun was situated at 1 entry, 58 Ghati and 3.87 Pal Decimal of Paush month.

Note, the difference between Nirayan month decimal 8.24 and Sayan month decimal 9.03 is 9.03-8.24=0.79 Bhukta season change month decimal. This shows the initial period of seasonal change.

Current Sayan Sun:- By adding Nirayan 8.24 to the current Ayanamsh 0.79 Rashi decimal, the Sayan Sun becomes known. Or consider the above Sayan Samvat month decimal also as Rashi decimal, by multiplying the digit after the decimal by 30, we get degree decimal, by multiplying the digit after the decimal by 60, we get minute decimal. Second decimals are obtained by multiplying the digit after the decimal by 60.

Calculation:- 8.24+0.79=9.03 Rashi (Capricorn) decimal, 0.03×30=0.97 Ansh decimal, 0.97×60=58.06 Kala decimal, 0.06×60=3.87 Vikala decimal were obtained. In annual motion, the Sayan Sun was situated in the degrees of Capricorn, 58 minute and 3.87 second decimal. See the above table, Shishir Ritu and Uttarayan are being known from the position of Sayan Sun in Capricorn.

Method of bringing Ganavarsha from Vikrami and Shaka Samvat:- In some previous chapter, Ganavarsha 1702.75 was found by subtracting Ayanamsh Shunyavrsha 320.22 from AD, there it was said that after finding Vikrami Samvat and Shaka Samvat, Ganavarsha can also be brought from the said Samvats. Ayanamshadhi calculations can be done, hence the Ganavarsha calculation method is being given here with an example. By subtracting Vikrami Ayanamsh minus 377 years from the current Vikram Samvat year decimal and including the current seasonal change year with decimal, Ganavarsha is obtained. Similarly, by subtracting Shaka Ayanamsh minus 242 years from the current Shaka Samvat year decimal, Ganavarsha is obtained.

Example:- Vikrami Samvat decimal of 22nd December 2023 AD was obtained as 2079.69-377=1702.69 Varshadi, which is without seasonal change, hence by adding the seasonal change year decimal that occurred during the said period to 1702.69 Varshadi, Ganavarsha is obtained. Season change till the above period, adding 0.07 years decimal to 1702.69, yielded 1702.75 years. To get Ganavarsha from Shaka Samvat, Shaka Samvat decimal of 22 December 2023 AD was obtained as 1944.75-242=1702.75 Ganavarsha.

Hari Om

CHAPTER NINE

KALISAMVAT (ERA) DECISION

Refinement Year Decimal: Make the month decimal by dividing the season change day etc. by the average Nirayan month. Similarly, make the month of 21st March a decimal and add both, if the sum is more than 12 then subtract 12 and divide by 12 to get the year decimal.

Refinement Year Calculation:- In the 152nd Chakra, the seasonal change till 22nd December 2023 AD was 24.13 days and the Ishtavarsha was 2022.97 years, on converting it into month decimal, 0.79 month (0.07 years) decimal is obtained and the month decimal of 21st March is 2.65. . Seasonal change month 0.79+2.65 (21 March)=3.44 month decimals were obtained, dividing them by 12 made year decimals, 3.44/12=0.29 refinement year decimals were obtained.

To find Kali Samvat:- Subtract the Shodha year decimal from the current Ishta year, after adding 3101 years to the obtained remainder, the present Kaliyuga Samvat year decimal is obtained. Or by including 3044.09 years in the decimal of the current year of Vikrami Samvat and subtracting 0.09 years of seasonal change, the decimal of Kali Samvat year is obtained. Or adding 3179.22 years to the current Shaka Samvat and subtracting 0.29 years of seasonal change from the beginning of Kali to the present, Kali Samvat is obtained.

In year decimal, month decimals are obtained by multiplying the post-decimal digit by 12, entry decimals are obtained by multiplying the post-decimal digit by the days of the respective month, ghati decimals are obtained by multiplying the post-decimal digit by 60. The pal decimals are obtained by multiplying the digit after the decimal by 60.

Calculation:-Current Ishtavarsha 2022.97-0.29=2022.69+3101=5123.69 years decimal orThe present Vikrami Samvat 2079.69+3044.09-0.09=5123.69 years decimal or the present Shaka Samvat 1944.75+3179.22-0.29=5123.69 years decimal Kali Samvat was obtained. In the year decimal, the decimal later digits were obtained 0.69×12=8.24 Paush month decimal, 0.24×30=7.18 Pravishte decimal, 0.18×60=10.9 Ghati decimal, 0.9×60=54.13 Pal decimal.

From the beginning of Kaliyuga till present (22 December 2023 AD), 5123 years of Kali Samvat have passed, in the 5124th Nirayan year of Kali Samvat, 8 entry, 10 ghati and 54.13 pal decimal of Paush month is going on.

Finding the date of the beginning of Kalisamvat: If the date from the beginning of 151st Chakra to the end of Dwaparayuga or the beginning of Kali is to be calculated by direct calculation from the AD pattern, then the seasonal change month till the end of Dwaparayuga will be in decimal 10.41 and the month of Sayan Kumbh Sankranti in decimal 0.61 (table below). See adding 11.02 month decimal (December) is obtained. Multiplying 0.02 digits after the decimal in December month decimal by the total 31 days of December gives 0.62 days or 1st December, which is the date of Nirayan Aquarius Sankranti at the end of Dwaparayuga. In this day, adding Kali Navasamvat 29 (28.43) and dividing it by the total 31 days of the month of December, 0.94 month decimal is obtained. By including the above 11.02 month decimal in the obtained month decimal 0.94, 11.96 month decimal (December) is obtained. In these monthly decimals, by multiplying the digits after the decimal with the total 31 days of December, the date of the end of Dwaparayuga or the beginning of Kaliyuga is obtained.

Example: Season change month decimal 10.41+0.61=11.02 December month decimal, digits after decimal 0.02×31=0.62 days or 1 December Nirayan Kumbh Sankranti day was obtained. Nirayan Kumbh Sankranti used to take place on 1st December during the end of Dwaparayuga or the beginning of Kali. For how many years did Nirayan Kumbh Sankranti happen on 1st December? This has been given in detail in Nirayan Sankranti chapter. 0.62+28.43=29.05/31=0.94 month, 0.94+11.02=11.96

December month decimal, 0.96×31=29.67 days or 30th December i.e. counting from the beginning of 151st Chakra, the date of end of Dwaparyug or beginning of Kaliyuga period was found to be 30th December.

The month of Sayan Sankranti is the decimal table					
Month	Sayan Sing	Season	N.Sign	Month	Sayan M.D.
March	Aquarius	Spring	Aries	Baishak	2.65
April	Pisces	Summer	Taurus	Jyestha	3.63
May	Aries	Summer	Gemini	Ashadh	4.65
June	Taurus	Monsoon	Cancer	Shravan	5.67
July	Gemini	Monsoon	Leo	Bhadrapada	6.71
August	Cancer	Autumn	Virgo	Ashwin	7.71
September	Leo	Autumn	Libra	Kartik	8.73
October	Virgo	Pre-Winter	Scorpio	Margshirsha	9.71
November	Libra	Pre-Winter	Sagittarius	Posh	10.70
December	Scorpio	Winter	Capricorn	Magh	11.68
January	Sagittarius	Winter	Aquarius	Phalgun	0.61
February	Capricorn	Spring	Pisces	Chaitra	1.64

Bringing the date of Kali Navasamvat in the present time:- Kaliyuga started on 30th December, so at present on which month or date the new year of Kalisamvat starts? It is very easy to find this out. By counting the seasonal change days from 30th December from the beginning of Kaliyuga to the present, the date of New Year Kalisamvat is obtained.

If you want to calculate in detail then first of all add the seasonal change days from the beginning of Kali Yuga till present and divide by the average of Sayan month and get the decimal of season change month. Seasonal change month, convert the above mentioned 11.96 December month decimal into decimal, then by multiplying the digits after the decimal with the days of the respective month (January etc.), decimals of the previous day are obtained. By including one extra day in it, the present Kalinavasamvad is clearly visible. The date is obtained. Hours decimal is obtained by multiplying the digit after the decimal by 24, minutes decimal is obtained by multiplying the digit after the decimal by 60.

Calculation:- Season change from the beginning of Kaliyuga to Zero Ayanamsha is 48.49 days and season change from Zero Ayanamsha year to present is 24.13 days, add 48.49+24.13=72.62 days, since the beginning of Kaliyuga till now there has been a seasonal change of 72.62 days. If these days are converted into months then 72.62/(365.24219/12)= 2.39 months (March) decimal, 2.39+11.96=14.34-12=2.34 March month decimal, digits after decimal 0.34×31=10.63 days decimal, 1 day more in this By combining, a clear date is obtained. 10.63+1=11.63 days or March 12, 0.63×24=15.22 hours decimal, 0.22×60=12.99 minutes decimal obtained. In the year 2024 AD, New Kalisamvat 5125th year will start from 15hrs., 12.99 minutes on 12th March. In the previous chapters Vikami and Shaka Samvat, pre and post and Nirayan and Sayan Surya, the beginning of Kaliyuga was said to be 29th entry of Phalgun solar month, which will always be on 29th entry of Phalgun month, whereas after 70.56 years in AD, the date increased by one day.

Attention! In this calculation, it has been asked to include one extra day in 10.63 days. Because when Nirayan is said, there is a difference of one day or a few hours or it is 28 Phalguna, but the type of calculation is correct. For clear calculation, the month decimal is obtained by dividing the Nirayan month decimal by 72.62 seasonal change days from the beginning of Kaliyuga to the present day. Days decimal is obtained by multiplying the digit after the decimal by 31. 72.62/(365.2429/12)=2.39 March, figures after decimal 0.39×31= 11.96 or 12 March, 0.96×24=23.12 hours, 0.12×60=7.25 minutes, clear Kalisamvat New Year date on 12 March at 23 hours and 7.25 minutes etc. Received.

Determining Kalisamvat period:- After subtracting 22349.91 Ishtavarshadis from Chakra, 3421.09 Varshadis were left at the end of Dwaparyuga. In these remaining years, the resolution of Ayanamsha from zero year till present. By adding Ganavarsha, the period of Kalisamvatkal is obtained. This Dwaparyug ending period is Kalisamvat period from the beginning of Phalgun month 29 till the present.

Keep in mind, if the said period is counted from Phalgun month, the month entries of Kali Samvat are known as Vikrami Samvat. Just as the month of Kalisamvat period is decimalized in the decimal of Phalgun month of the end of Dwaparayuga, by finding the day and date of the obtained month decimal, the current month and date are obtained.

Calculations:- Vikrami Samvat 2079.69-377=1702.69 Nirayana Ganavarsha, 3421.09+ 1702.69=5123.77 Kali Samvat period. Decimals after the digits 0.77×12=9.29 months decimals, 29×30=8.75 days, 0.75×24=17.95 hours, 0.95×60=57.04 minutes, etc., i.e., 22 December 2023, 4th Paush 2079 of the Kali Samvat period Year , 9months, 8days. 17 hours and 57.04 minutes have passed, these are the rainfall calculated considering the first month of the year in the month of Falgun (29 Pravisthe). If we want to know the past months and so on according to Vikrmi Samvat, then the end of Dwapara Yuga is the month decimal 10.95+9.29=20.24-12=8.24 month decimal, 0.24×30=7.18 days, 0.18×60=10.90 ghati, 0.90×60=54.13 pal etc., this is of the present Vikrami Samvat 8th of Paush.

Let us take an example of March 12, 2024, at 23:07, 7.19 minutes (Vikrami Ishtavarsh 2079.91), on this day 5124 years of Kali Samvat were completed. By including the years from the beginning of Kali to the middle of the beginning of Vikami in the Ishtavarsha decimal of March 12, 2024, the last Kalisamvat period is obtained as 2079.91+3421.09= 5124.00. We find out the Month etc. of Vikrami Samvat Ishtavarsha 2079.91 years, 0.91×12=10.95 month decimal, 0.95×30=28.44 days or 29 entries were received i.e. on 12 March 2023 AD, on the 29th entry day of Vikami 2080 Samvat Phalguna month, 5124 days of Kalisamvat period. Years are over.

Note, the question here may be that when 29 entries of Phalgun arrive every year, it would already be known that it is the new year of Kalisamvat, then why was the Kalisamvat period calculated separately? In response to this, I would like to say that I tried to display the complete years of the New Year, Ahargana separately on the excel sheet, for this I worked by applying the IF formula but did not get satisfaction, due to the mismatch of digits after the decimal, there was a delay of a few minutes. Complete years were being displayed from 1250 onwards, so for calculating Kalisamvat, Phalgun was considered as the first year of the month. The above calculation was done considering the month and it was successful.

Date of beginning of Kali Yuga in BC:- Kali Yuga started 3101 years after the beginning of Kali Yuga, or Kali Yuga started in 3101 BC from the beginning of AD. Therefore, by multiplying 3101 years by the days of the two Nirayana and Sayan Surya years, the days of seasonal change etc. are obtained. Or by multiplying 3101 by the days of Nirayan year and dividing it by Chakra, the days of seasonal change are obtained.

Make the year a decimal by dividing the seasonal change days by the average Sayan month and then divide by 12 and add it to 3101 years. By multiplying the post-decimal digit in the said year decimal by 12, the month decimal is obtained, by multiplying the post-decimal digit by the days of the respective month (January etc.), the previous date decimal is obtained, by multiplying the post-decimal digit by 24, But hours are obtained as decimals, minutes are obtained as decimals by multiplying the digit after the decimal by 60.

Calculation: If we distinguish between 3101×365.256363=1132659.98 days and 3101×365.24219=1132616.03 days, 1132659.98(-)1132616.03=43.95 season change days were obtained or 3101×365.256363/25771=43.95 season change days, 43.95/(365.24219/12)/12=0.12 years decimal, 3101+0.12=3101.12 years decimal, digits after decimal 0.12×12=1.44 (February) month Decimal, 0.44×28=12.43 days decimal, decimal 0.43×24= 10.37 hours decimal, decimal 0.36×60=22.27 minutes decimal. Kaliyuga started at 10hrs., 22.27 minute am on 13 February 3102 BC.

Note, the midnight of 17th/18th February BC is considered to be the beginning of Kaliyuga. If we include the seasonal change days of last year 320 AD (Ayanamsh zero year) in the above mentioned 13th February, then from the above calculation, 17th February is coming, but then it would be appropriate to call it 17th February since Ayanamsh zero year 3422.

I calculate and say, 3421×365.256363/25771=48.49 season change day,

48.49/(365.24219/12)/12=0.13 year decimal, 3421+0.13=3421.13 year decimal, 0.13×12= 1.59 (February) month decimal, 0.59×28=16.60 days decimal, digits after decimal 0.60×24=14.51 hours decimal, digits after decimal 0.51×60=30.37 minutes decimal. Kaliyuga started on 17th February 3422 years before Ayanamsha Shunyavarsha at 14hrs., 30.37 minutes.

Here, if we want to say BC, then Kaliyuga will be said to have started at 14hrs, 30.37 minutes on 17th February 3102 BC, because if you count the beginning of Kaliyuga from the current date of 22nd December, 2023 BC, then from the present, BC will be started. The period till the beginning will disappear, your statement would be correct only after adding the remaining 3101 years and the seasonal changes that occurred during this period. In the calculation of 17/18 February, the seasonal change till Ayanamsh is being taken as zero year, which is definitely 3102 years if we say BC.

Here, if the reverse calculation is done from the present to Kalistart period in the above manner, then the present. There has been a seasonal change of 72.62 days from 1000 BC to Kaliprambh, on this basis, 12 March 3102 BC will be called Kaliprambh, whereas here it would be appropriate to say that Kaliyuga started on 12 March 5124th year before the current date 22 December 2023 AD. Therefore, the truth which is obtained through calculations has been placed in front of you.

According to the conclusion:- It is appropriate to call 13th February 3102 BC as the beginning of Kaliyuga. If Ayanamsha zero is to be said from 3421 years then 17th February should be said to be the beginning of Kaliyuga 3422 years ago.

Brief:-

In earlier chapters, the Shodhana years were determined at two places, the Shodhana year of the end of Dwaparayuga was 0.09 years decimal and the present Shodhana year was 0.29 decimals, if they are differentiated then the seasonal change from the beginning of Kaliyuga to the present would be 0.20 years or 2.39 months or 72.62 days decimal. Is. Apart from this, if we subtract 0.22 (21st March) years decimal from 0.29 years decimal, then 0.07 years decimal season change from Ayanamsha zero time till present is obtained.

• Ishtavarsha is Sayan, hence the distance between the beginning of Kaliyuga from the beginning of AD period is taken to be 3101 years, Vikrami is Nirayan, hence the distance from the beginning of Kaliyuga to the beginning of Vikrami period is taken to be 3044.09 years.

• According to Nirayan Samvat, Kaliyuga started on 29th (28.43) of Phalgun solar month. Every year, Kalisamvat New Year will begin on 29th Pravisht of Phalgun. But the above Kali Navasamvat date is currently 12th March and will become 13th March after completion of 70.56 years.

• Why is Kalisamvat being expressed from Vikrami Samvat only? Why not from AD? To express time, one has to say Samvat year, month and entry or year, month and date. Here Kalisamvat has been expressed from Vikrami Samvat. The main reason for this is the seasonal change, if any period is expressed in terms of sayan years then it is inferior to the seasonal change of that period. Nirayana is stable, due to seasonal changes in it, there is a continuous addition of time period.

• Just as the years of Kali Samvat are differentiated by multiplying them by the days of Nirayan and Sayan year, this difference is the seasonal change from the beginning of Kali Samvat to the present Kali Nava Samvat. 5123.69×365.256363=1871459.14 Nirayan Ahargan Kaliyug begins, 5123.69×365.24219=1871386.52 Sayan Ahargan Kaliyug begins, the difference between the two is 72.62 days, which is the seasonal change day from the beginning of Kaliyug to 22 December 2023 AD.

The seasonal change from the beginning of Kaliyuga is 48.49 days and the seasonal change from Zero Ayanamsha year till present is 24.13 days. Since the beginning of Kaliyuga till now, 72.62 days of seasonal change have taken place. Now you think for yourself, if we stick to the date of Kalisamvat or any other historical festival from Sayan date (January etc.), then after many years, there will be a difference of many days by a multiple of 70.56 years. Therefore, festivals should be celebrated only on the dates associated with seasonal changes. In our mountains, earlier festivals like birthdays etc. were celebrated only with the entry of Nirayan Surya Sankranti.

Hari Om

CHAPTER TEN

AHARGANA AND VAAR

In the chapter Ahargana and Vaar, we will find out Vaar by taking out Ahargana from the beginning of Kaliyuga, Ayanamsha zero year and till the present. Apart from this, we will find out Vaar by taking out Ahargana from the beginning of Kaliyuga till Ayanamsha zero year and present. We will also find out the days on the basis of Gregorian calendar.

Ahargana and Vaar after Satyayuga to Dwaparant:- There are 432000×9=3888000 years from Satyuga to Dwaparant, by multiplying the said years by the days of Sayan year i.e. 365.24219, Ahargana is obtained, divide the obtained Ahargana by 7, sacrifice the obtained gain. The number is known by taking the tax balance and multiplying it by 7 and counting the product till its integer.

3888000×365.24219=1420061634.72 days, Ahargana days obtained from Satyayuga to the end of Dwaparayuga. Divided by 7 in these days 1420061634.72/7=202865947.82 weeks etc. Result decimal, digits after decimal 0.82×7=5.72 days decimal, integer 6 Sunday...1, Monday..2, Tuesday..3, Wednesday.. 4, Thursday..5 and Friday...6. Starting **Friday** of Kaliyuga was obtained from integer 6.

Ahargana and Vaar from Satyayuga to Ayanamsha Shunyavarsha: The days from Satyayuga to Ayanamsha Shunyavarsha are 151×25771=3891421 years, because during this period the seasonal change of 0.22 years (0.09+0.13=0.22) decimal was also completed. Hence, include 0.22 years in the above mentioned years, multiply the obtained sum of 3891421.22 by the days of the year i.e. 365.24219 to get the Ahargana, divide the obtained Ahargana by 7, discard the obtained gain, take the remainder and multiply it by 7. The number is known by counting the obtained product till its integer.

3891421.22×365.24219=1421311208.76 days, Ahargana days from Satyuga to Ayanamsha Shunyavarsha day Received. Divided by 7 on these days 1421311208.76/7=203044458.39 weeks etc. Result decimal, digits after decimal 0.39×7=2.76 days decimal, integer 3 Sunday..1, Monday...2 and Tuesday..3, integer 3 Ayanamsha was obtained on **Tuesday** of the zero year day.

Current Ahargana and Vaar from Satyayuga:- Present day from Satyayuga is 151×25771= 3891421 years, add current Ganavarsha 1702.75 in the said years, the obtained sum is obtained by multiplying 3893123.97 years with 365.24219 days of Sayan year, Ahargana is obtained. Divide by 7, discard the result, take the remainder, multiply it by 7 and count the product till its integer, the number is known.

3893123.97×365.24219=1421933125.88 days, the number of days received from Satyayuga to present. Divided by 7 on these days 1421933125.88/7=203133303.70 Weeks etc. Result decimal, digits after decimal 0.70×7=4.88 times decimal, integer 5 on Sunday...1, Monday..2, Tuesday..3., Wednesday..4 and Thursday..5. The integer 5 gives the current day's **Thursday**, which is one day less than the current day's Friday.

Ahargana and Vaar from the beginning of Kaliyuga to Ayanamsha Shunyavarsha: To find out the days from the beginning of Kaliyuga to Ayanamsha Shunyavarsha, decimalize the year of 21st March (0.09+0.13=0.22) in 3421 years, 3421+0.22=3421.22 years are obtained. By multiplying the above mentioned years by the days of the Sayan year i.e. 365.24219, Ahargana is obtained, divide the obtained Ahargana by 7, after discarding the obtained gain, take the remainder and convert it into 7.

The number is known by counting the product obtained by multiplying it till its integer. 3421.22×365.24219=1249574.04 days were obtained from Kaliyuga to Ayanamsha Zerotime. Divided by 7 in these days 1249574.04/7=178510.58 Weeks etc. Result decimal, digits after decimal 0.58×7=4.04 times decimal, integer 5 Friday..1, Saturday..2, Sunday..3, Monday..4 And Tuesday..5, from the integer 5, **Tuesday** of the day of Ayanamsha Shunyavarsha was obtained.

Ahargana and Vaar from the beginning of Kali to the present: To find out the days from the beginning of Kali to the present, add 21st March of the current Kali Samvat Varshadi in decimal and the current season change with 0.07 years decimal (0.09+0.13+0.07=0.29), 5123.69+0.29=Received 5123.97 years. By multiplying the above mentioned years by the days of the Sayan year i.e. 365.24219, Ahargan is obtained, divide the obtained Ahargan by 7, after discarding the obtained gain, take the remainder and multiply it by 7 and count the product till its integer from Friday. The **attack** becomes known.

Calculation:- 5123.97×365.24219=1871491.16 days, Kaliyahargan days obtained from Kaliyuga to present. Divided by 7 on these days 1871491.16/7=267355.88 weeks etc. Result decimal, digits after decimal 0.88×7=6.16 times decimal, integer 7 on Friday..1, Saturday..2, Sunday...3, Monday.. 4, Tuesday. 5. Wednesday...6 and Thursday..7. From integer 7, **Thursday** of the day of Ayanamsha Shunyavarsha was obtained, which is one day less than Friday of this day.

Kalikaalavadhi Ahargana and Vaar: By including the present Nirayan 1702.69 Ganavarsha in the Bhogya Nirayan 3421.09 years from the beginning of Kali to the middle of Ayanamsh Shunyavarsha, the Kaliprambha period is obtained. By multiplying the said period by the days of the Nirayan year, clear Ahargana Vaar is obtained, if the said period is If we multiply it by the days of the Sayan year and differentiate it from the obvious Ahargana, then these are the days of seasonal change from the beginning of Kali to the present.

Calculation:- 3421.09+1702.69=5123.77 Kalikaalavadhi, 5123.77×365.24219=1871418.55 days, Kaliahargan days from Kaliyuga till present were obtained. Divided by 7 in these days 1871418.55/ 7=267345.51 Weeks etc. Result Decimal, digits after decimal 0.51×7=3.55 wise decimal, integer 4 Friday.. 1. Saturday..2, Sunday..3, Monday..4 , from the integer 4, the day wise of Ayanamsh Shunyavarsha, **Monday** is obtained, which is four days less than this day wise Friday. The reason for this is that Kalikalavadhi is a Nirayana calculation, Nirayana is free from seasonal change, if we differentiate between the two aharganas of Kali and Kalikalavadhi, then we will get seasonal change of 1871491.16-1871418.55=72.62 days.

Gregorian Calendar:- In earlier times, Ahargana calculation was done from the beginning of creation or Kaliyuga or from a certain Shaka Samvat to the desired Shaka Samvat, but in the present time, due to the greater prevalence of AD year, Ahargana calculation is done from AD year. Which is popular in most of the countries because it is simple, convenient and practical, but because it is full of tricks, it never matches with the pure Vedic wise.

The Christian era started with the estimated birth date of Isha as the basis. Initially a year of 304 days was considered, in which there were 10 months from March to December. But later, by amending it, January and February were extended by two more months to make it 354 days equivalent to the lunar year. 45 years before Isha, Emperor Julius Caesar also amended it and made it based on the solar year. In this Julian calendar, every 4th year was considered a leap year, due to which disparity started appearing between the solar year and the solar year-based Julian calendar. In 1582 AD, the 13th Pope Gregory of Rome made many amendments and gave it a new form of the Gregorian calendar. First of all, by considering 4th October as 15th October, he corrected the inaccuracy of 11 days already and made it completely based on the solar year.

He assumed a long cycle of 400 years, which has a total of 146097 days. After the end of a long cycle, the attacks recur on the fixed dates of the new long cycle, that is, after 400 years of one long cycle have passed, the same attacks occur on the same dates in the new long cycle. This long cycle is complemented by four medium cycles of 100 years each. In which three medium cycles end normally and one medium cycle ends with Leep Year. There are a total of 36524 days in the 100 years of a normal Midile Cycle and 36525 days in the 100 years of Leep Midile Cycle. Thus, General Madhyam Chakra 3×36524=109572 days+36525 days of Laundh Madhyam Chakra makes a Long Chakra of 146097 days. Apart from this, short cycles of 4-4 years were imagined, one short cycle consists of 1461 days.

In a short cycle of 4 years, the first, second and third years are normal i.e. of 365 days each and every fourth year is a Leep year, which has 366 days. Thus, 3 years of normal years × 365=1095 days+366 days of Lunar year=1461 days in a short cycle. In a normal year, February has 28 days and in a leap year, February has 29 days. The rule of status quo was made in the hundred times of the normal and leap years of the short cycle, that is, like 1, 2, 3 normal years, $1 \times 100 = 100^{th}$ year, $2 \times 100 = 200^{th}$ year, $3 \times 100 = 300^{th}$ year. There will be normal years and like the 4th Leep year, the $4 \times 100 = 400^{th}$ year will be the year of Leep. In this way, in a long cycle, the three medium cycles will end as normal and the fourth medium cycle will end as Leep year.

There are 365 days, 5 hours, 48 minutes, and 45.216 seconds in a solar year (365.24219 days). A Short Cycle is completed by three normal and one leap years, there are 365 days in a normal year and 366 days in a leap year. Thus, a minor cycle is of $365.24219 \times 4 = 1460.96876$ days but to give parity it is taken to be 1461 days. Due to which in each short cycle 1461 (-) 1460.96876 = 0.03124 days or 44 min 59.136 sec are exceeded and in 100 years $100/4 = 25 \times 0.03124 = 0.781$ days or 18 hrs 44 min 38.4 sec, in 200 years $200/4 = 50 \times 0.03124 = 1.562$ days or 1 day 13 hours 29 minutes 16.8 seconds, in 300 years $300/4 = 75 \times 0.03124 = 2.343$ days or 2 days 8 hours 13 minutes 55.2 seconds. This Extra Days is established by reducing one day each from the ending years of the normal medium cycles i.e. 100th, 200th and 300th year. Because in 100 years there were 0.781 days (18 hours 44 minutes 38.4 seconds) more but one day was reduced there, thus in 400 years 1 (-) $0.781 \times 4 = 0.876$ days or 21 hours 1 minute 26.4 seconds less. Become. This is accomplished by increasing one day in the 400th year of a long cycle. It is noteworthy that the Christian era starts from 1st January and ends on 31st December and 1st January 0001 AD is considered as Monday.

After 400 years of each long cycle, 1(-)0.876=0. 124 days or 2h 58m 33.6s are increasing. On this basis $1/0.124 \times 400 = 3225.8064$. There will be one more day in 3225.80645161 years. What will be the arrangements for this long day..? It is in the womb of the future.

To find the Vaar:- Subtract the desired AD year by the multiplier of 400. Divide the remainder by 100, write the quotient separately, call it quotient 1, and divide the remainder by 4. Add the quotient 2 to the quotient-1, write it separately, and multiply it by 5. Add whatever was left after dividing by 4. In the total obtained, add the desired date and the polar number of the desired month and divide the remainder by 7. If it is a leap year, if it is a normal year, then Ishtavar is obtained by counting from Saturday. pay attention. Understand if the remainder remains zero after subtracting by multiples of 400 or dividing by 4.It is a leap year.

Example-1:- Let us find the date of 15th August 1947. After reducing the desired year 1947 AD by a factor of 400, the remainder was 347/100=3 quotient (quotient-1), the remainder was 47/4=11 quotient (quotient 2), the remainder was 3, sum of quotients one and two and multiplied by 5, 3+11×5=70 product, adding both the sum results and multiplying by 5, the product is 70.

On dividing by four, the remainder was 3+70=73, to this 73 the pole number of August of the common year was added 73+2=75, to this sum 75 the auspicious date was added, the sum was 75+15=90. It was divided by 7, the result was 90/7=12, the remaining 6 were counted from Sunday's minimum to 6 and Friday was obtained.

Mass Druvank		
Mass	Normal year	Leap year
January	0	0
February	3	3
March	3	4
April	6	0
May	1	4
June	4	5
July	6	2
August	2	3
September	5	6
October	0	1
November	3	4
December	5	6

Example-2:- Let us find the day of 1 January 2000 AD. By subtracting the desired year 2000 AD by a factor of 400, the remainder was 0, hence it is a leap year. Remainder 0+100=0 quotient (quotient-1), remainder 0÷4=0 quotient (quotient-2), remainder remained, quotient one and two were added and multiplied by 5, 0+0×5=0 product, By combining both the sums and multiplying them by 5, the result was 0.

On dividing by four, the remainder was 0+00=0, to this 0 the pole number of January leap year was added 0+0=0, to this sum 0 the auspicious date was added, the sum was 0+1=1. It was divided by 7, the result was 1/7=0, the remainder 1 was counted from less than 1 of Saturday and Saturday was obtained.

Example-3:- Let us find the date of March 17, 2012. After subtracting the desired year 2012 by a multiplier of 400, the remainder is 12, the remainder is 12/100=0, quotient (quotient 1), the remainder is 12/4=3 quotient (quotient-2), the remainder is 0, hence it is a leap year. Quotient one and two are added and multiplied by 5, 0+3×5=15 product, By combining both the sums and multiplying them by 5, the result was 15.

On dividing by four, the remainder was 0+15=15, to this 15, the pole number of March leap year was added, 15+4=19, to this sum 19, the auspicious date was added, the sum was 19+17=36. It was divided by 7, the result was 36/7=5, by counting the remainder 1 from the less than 1 of Saturday, Saturday was obtained.

Example-4:- Let us find the date of 22nd December 2023. After reducing the desired year 2023 AD by a factor of 400, the remainder is 23/100=0, quotient-1, the remainder is 23/4=5, quotient-1, the remainder is 3, sum quotient one and two and multiply by 5. Did, 0+5×5=25 product, adding both the sum results and multiplying by 5, got 25 product.

On dividing by four, the remainder was 3+25=28, to this 28, the polar number of December of the common year was added, 28+5=33, to this sum 33, the auspicious date was added, the sum was 33+22=55. Dividing it by 55/7=7 resulted in the remaining 6 being counted from the lowest 6 of Sunday to Friday.

Hari Om

CHAPTER ELEVEN

ONE DEGREE AYANAMSH'S BHUKTA AND BHOGYA YEARS ETC.

The absolute temporal value of one Ansh Ayanamsh is 71.59 years. How many years has the victim passed in the middle of Ayanamsha calculation? How many years are left?... It is also necessary to know this or have knowledge of this. To make this calculation, by subtracting the previous Ayanamsh fractions from the current Ayanamsh fractions and multiplying it by 71.59 years, Bhukta years are obtained. Subtract the current Ayanamsha from its whole number, multiply the remainder by 71.59 years to get the Bhogya years. The starting time of Ayanamsha parts is known by subtracting the Bhukta from the Ishtavarshas like present Vikrami, Shaka or Eesan and the ending time is known by including the Bhogya in the Ishtavarshas.

If the said Bhukta Bhogya years are to be calculated before Christ, then by adding the Bhukta years to 3101.0 years, the starting period of one Ansh Ayanamsha will be obtained and by subtracting the Bhogya years from 3101.0 years, the ending time of one Ansh Ayanamsh will be obtained.

If the year and Month etc. are to be determined through precise calculations, then keep in mind that Bhukta-Bhogya Varshaadi containing decimals are indicators of previous years, like in the Ishtavarsha pattern of the end of Dwapar Yuga or the beginning of Kaliyuga, Vikami is 22349.91 Gatvarshadi, Shaka Samvat is 22349.78 Gatvarshadi and A.D. There are 22350 previous years, hence there are 22351 current years, under which Ishtamas, Days etc. have to be expressed.

Note, there is no Paisa Samvat before and after Kalikal (3044 years), which is still in circulation. But Nirayan and Sayan solar years are always there, so that confusion does not arise, I am addressing Nirayan's pattern as Vikami, Sayan's pattern as Shaka and AD.

By multiplying the digits (remainder) after the decimal by 12, we get the month of January etc., multiplying the remainder with the total days of the respective month of January etc., we get the date, by multiplying the remainder by 24, we get hours, Multiplying the remainder by 60 gives minutes and multiplying the remainder by 60 gives seconds.

By multiplying the digits after the decimal (remainder) by 12, the months of Baishakhadi and Chaitradi are obtained respectively, the remainder is multiplied by the total days of the respective month to get the entry, by multiplying the remainder by 60, the Ghati is obtained. Multiplying the remainder by 60 gives Pal and multiplying the remainder by 60 gives Vipal.

Example :-

AD Pattern (A-Ganavarsha, Bhukta Varshadi): The Ayanamsha of the beginning of Kaliyuga was at 312.21 degrees. Hence, multiplying the remainder of 312.21-312=0.21 by 71.59 years gives 0.21×71.59=15.13 spent years. If these Bhukta years were subtracted from the 22350 Ishtavarshas, we got 22350.0-15.13=22334.87 years. In the 22334.87th year of the 151st Sayan Chakra, the 312th part ended or the 313th part started.

0.87 × 12 = 10.4 months (November), remaining 0.4 × 30 (November) = 12 days, obtained on 13 November, that is, in the 22335th year of 151st Sayan Chakra, the 313th degree started from 00:00 AM on 13th November.

Bhogya Varshadih:- 312.21 degrees were subtracted from 313 degrees and multiplied by 71.59 years, then 313-312.21 = 0.79 degrees, 0.79×71.59 = 56.45 years were obtained. This was added to 22350, after

22350+56.45=22406.45 years the 313th fraction was completed. 0.45×12=5.43 months (June), remainder 0.43×30=13 days (14th June), remainder 0 obtained i.e. end of 313th degree at 00:00, 00 minutes and 0.0 seconds on 14th June in the 22407th year of 151st Sayan Chakra.

Vikami Pattern (A-Ganavarsha, Bhukta Varshadi): By subtracting 15.13 Spent years from 22349.91 Ishtavarshas, we get 22349.91-15.13=22334.78 years, 312th part in 22334.78[th] Nirayan year of 151st Sayan Chakra.

Had it ended or had the 313th part started? The digits after the decimal are 0.78×12=9.35 months (Magh), the remaining 0.35×30 (Magh)=10.43 entries, 11 entries of Magh month were obtained, that is, in the 22335th year of the 151st Sayan Chakra, the 313th degree started from 11 Magh.

Bhogya Varshadhi:- 56.45 Bhogya Varsha, added it to 22349.91, 313th part completed after 22349.91+56.45=22406.37 years. 0.37×12=4.38 months (Bhadrapada), remaining 0.38×30= 11.43 entries (12 Bhadrapada) i.e. 313th part ended on 12 Bhadrapada in the 22407th year of 151st Sayan Chakra.

Shaka Pattern (A-Ganavarsha, Bhukta Varshadi): 15.13 Spent years, subtracting these spent years from 22349.78 Ishtavarshas gives 22349.78-15.13=22334.65 years, 312th part ended in 22334.65[th] Sayan year of 151st Sayan Chakra or 313th The portion had started. 0.65×12=7.75 month (Kartik), digits after decimal 0.75×30=22.65 entries, 23 entries Sayan Kartik month was obtained i.e. 313th degree started from 23 Kartik in the 22335th year of 151st Sayan Chakra.

Bhogya Varshadih- 56.45 Bhogya Varsha, added it to 22349.78, 313th part completed after 22349.78+56.45=22406.23 years. 0.23×12=2.79 months (Jyeshtha), remaining 0.79×31= 24.43 entries (25 Jyeshtha) i.e. in the 22407th year of 151st Sayan Chakra, the 313th part ended on 25 Jyeshtha.

Samvat Bhukta Table			
	Spent year	Month	Days
AD pattern	22334.87	10.40 (November)	13
Vikrami pattern	22334.78	9.35 (Magh)	11
Shaka Pattern	22334.65	7.75 (Kartik)	23

Samvat Bhogya Table			
	Bhogya year	Month	Days
AD pattern	22406.45	5.43 (June)	14
Vikrami pattern	22406.37	4.38 (Bhadrapad)	12
Shaka Pattern	22406.23	2.79 (Jyestha)	25

Ganavarshaadi Bhukta-Bhogya Table.		
	(a) Ganavarsha	(b) Ganavarsha
Bhukta/Bhogya	**316.77 Bhukta**	**48.49 Bhogya**
Season Change	0.87/0.09	0.13
Mass	10.41	1.59
Entries	12.39	18.05

Season difference table		
	Bhukta year	Month
AD pattern	22334.87	10.40 (November)
Vikrami pattern	22334.78	9.35 (January)
R.P. difference	0.09	1.05 (1.05/12=0.09)
Vikrami pattern	22334.78	9.35 (Magh)
Shaka Pattern	22334.65	7.75 (Kartik)
R.P. difference	0.13	1.59 (1.59/12=0.13)
AD pattern	22334.87	10.40 (November)
Shaka Pattern	22334.65	7.75 (Kartik)
R.P. difference	0.22	2.64 (2.64/12=0.22)

Confirmation:- In the above Samvat Bhokta-Bhogya table, the calculation of free Bhogya Varshadi of one degree ayanamsha has been tabulated. To confirm the calculation, first of all take a look at the seasonal change Bhukta 0.09 Varshadi / 10.41 month and Bhogya 0.13 Varshadi / 1.59 month in the Ganavarsha Bhukta-Bhogya table given below.

See the above season difference table, the difference of season change between AD 22334.87 Varshadi and Vikrami Samvat pattern 22334.78 Varshadi is 0.09 Varshadi, which is the seasonal change Varshadi till the end of Dwaparayuga, hence the calculation is confirmed. By the end of

Dwaparyuga, 316.77 days of seasonal change had passed, counting from at least 9.35 (10th) month of Baishakhadi, the month of November is also found under Magh month. In the table itself, the seasonal change difference between 22334.78 Varshadhi pattern Vikrami Samvat and 22334.65 Varshadhi per Shaka Samvat is 0.13 Varshadhi, which is the seasonal change Varshadhi from Kali start to Ayanamsh zero time, hence the re-calculation is confirmed. By the time of Ayanamsh Shunyakaal, 48.49 days of seasonal change had been consumed, counting from Baishakhadi month till 9.35 (10th) month gives Magha month and Chaitradhi month from at least 7.75 (8th) month, Sayan Kartik month is obtained. The difference between seasonal changes of both the months is 1.59 months decimal.

In the table itself, the difference of seasonal change of 22334.87 years pattern AD and 22334.65 years pattern Shaka Samvat is 0.22 years (0.09+0.13), which is the seasonal change of years from the beginning period of 151st Chakra till Ayanamsh zero period, hence the recalculation is confirmed. Is. From the beginning of 151st Chakra till Ayanamsh Shunyakaal, 365.256363 days of seasonal change had been suffered. By counting from January etc. at least till 10.4 (11th) month, November month is obtained and by counting from Chaitradhi month till 7.75 (8th) month, Sayan Kartik month is obtained. The difference in seasonal change of both the months is 2.64 months (20 March) decimal.

1. **BC (Spent Year):** 3101+15.13=3116.13 BC The 313th part started. 0.13×12 = 1.6 months (February), remainder 0.6×28 = 16.8 days (17 February), remainder 0.8×24=19.20 hours, remainder 0.20×60 = 12 minutes, remainder 0.00×60=00.00 seconds were obtained i.e. 3117 BC, The 313th part started at 19hrs, 12minutes and 00 seconds on 17 February.

2. **BC (Bhogya year):** -3101-56.45=3044.55 BC The 313th degree ended. 0.55×12= 6.57 months (July), remainder 0.57×31=17.57 days (18 July), remainder 0.57×24= 13.6 hours, remainder 0.6×60= 36 minutes, remainder 0 obtained i.e. 3045 BC, 18 July at 13 o'clock , 36 minutes and 00.00 seconds, But the 313th part ended.

3. **Vikrami Purva (Spent Year):-** 3044.09+15.13=3059.22 The 313th part of Vikrami Samvat Purva started. 0.22×12=2.65 months (Ashadha),

remainder 0.65×32=20.87 entries (21 Ashadha), remainder 0.87×60=52.24 Ghati, remaining 0.24×60=14.36 pal, remaining 0.36×60=21.50 Vipal were obtained i.e. 313th degree had started from 52Ghati, 14 Pal and 21 Vipal on 21st Ashadh of 3060th Vikrami Samvat.

4. **Vikrami Purva** (Bhogya Year):- 3044.09-56.45=2987.63 The 313th part of Vikrami Samvat Purva ended. 0.63×12=7.62 months (Margashirsha), remainder 0.62×30=18.57 Pravisthe (19 Margashirsha), remainder 0.57×60=33.97 ghati, remainder 0.97×60=58.46 pal, remainder 0.46×60=27.66 Vipal, received i.e. 2988th Vikrami Samvat Earlier, on the 19th day of Margashirsha month, the 313th part ended at 33 Ghati, 58 Pal and 27.66 vipaladi.

5. **Shaka Purva (Spent Year)**:- 3179.22+15.13=3194.35 Shaka Samvat Purva 313th part started. The digits after the decimal are 0.35×12=4.25month (Shravan), remaining 0.25×30= 7.6 Pravistha (8 Shravan), remaining 0.6×60=36.0 Ghati, remaining 0.0×60=0.00 pal, remaining 0.00×60=0.0 Vipal, i.e. 3195th Shaka Samvat Purva 8th Shravan started the 313th Ansh from 36 Ghati, 00 Pal and 00 Vipal.

6. **Shaka Purva (Bhogya year)**:- 3179.22-56.45=3122.77 Shaka Samvat Purva 313th part ended. Decimal figures 0.77×12=9.21 months (Paush), Decimal figures 0.21×30=6.35 entries (7 Paush), remainder 0.35×60=21.29 Ghati, remainder 0.29×60=17.42 pal, remainder 0.42×60=25.17 Vipals were received i.e. 3123rd Shaka Samvat Purva, 7th entry Paush month, 21 Ghati, 17 Pal and 25.17 Vipaladi ended 313th Ansh.

Confirmation:- See the Samvat Difference Varshadi table below, the difference between BC and Vikrami Purva is 56.91 Varshadi, the difference between before Vikrami and before Shaka is 135.13 years, while the difference between BC and before Shaka is 78.22 Varshadi, which is Let's confirm the calculations.

AD (C-Ganavarsha, Bhukta Year):- The Ayanamsha of 22 December 2023 AD was at 23.79 degrees. Hence, 23.79-23=0.79, multiplying the remainder by 71.59 years gives 0.79×71.59= 56.27 years. These years are reduced from 2022.97 years in decimal equivalent to the year of 22 December 2023 AD, 2022.97-56.27=1966.7 years in decimal.

The 23rd degree ended and the 24th degree started. 0.7×12=8.41 months (September), remainder 0.41×30=12.35 days (13 September), remainder 0.35×24=8.52 hours, figures after decimal 0.52×60=30.97 minutes, remainder 0.97×60=58.05 seconds obtained , i.e. 13 September, the 24th degree started at 8:30 minutes and 58.05 seconds in 1967 AD.

Bhogya year:- Subtracted 23.79 years from 24 degrees and multiplied by 71.59 years, got 24-23.79=0.21 degree, digits after decimal 0.21×71.59=15.31 years. Added this to 2022.97, 24th part will be completed after 2022.97+15.31=2038.29 years.

0.29×12=3.45 months (April), remainder 0.45×30=13.35 days (April 14), remainder 0.35×24 =8.52 hours, digits after decimal 0.52×60=30.97 minutes, remainder 0.97×60=58.05 seconds. , that is, on April 14, 2039 A.D., the 24th degree will end and the 25th degree will begin at 8:30 AM and 58.05 seconds.

Vikrami Samvat Bhukta Varsha:- By subtracting the Bhukta years from the current Vikrami Samvat Ishtavarsha, the initial year of the fraction is obtained. For the completion of the part, the completion period of the part is obtained by adding the Bhogya years in the current Vikrami Samvat Ishtavarsha. In the same manner, in the Shaka Samvat also, the starting and ending period of the part can be determined by respectively subtracting and adding the Bhukta-Bhogya in the current Ishtavarsha.

Calculations: The 24th started in the present Vikrami Samvat 2079.69-56.27=2023.41 Samvat, 0.41×12=4.97 months (Bhadrapada), the remainder 0.97×31=29.21 Pravisthe (30 Bhadrapada), the remainder 0.21×60=12.84 ghati, the remainder 0.84×6=50.13pal, the decimal later digits were obtained 0.13×60=7.51 vipal, i.e. 30 Pravistha Bhadrapada, 2024th Vikrami Samvat 24th degree started from 12 Ghati, 50 Pal and 7.51 Vipal.

Bhogya Varsha:- 2079.69+15.31=2095.0006 Samvat Decimal will end the 24th part, decimal after digits 0.0006×12=0.01 month (Baisakh), decimal after digits 0.01×31=0.22Pravisthe (1 Baishakh), remainder 0.22×6=13.26 ghatis, remainder 0.26×60=15.80pals, remainder 0.80×60=47.77 vipals were obtained, i.e. 1 Pravistha Baisakh, 2096th Vikrami Samvat will start the 25th fraction from 13 ghatis, 15 pals and

47.77 vipals.

Shaka Bhukta Varsha:- The 24th began in the present Shaka Samvat 1944.75-56.27= 1888.48, the decimal after the digits 0.48×12=5.77 months (Bhadrapada), the remainder 0.77×31=23.77 Pravisthe (24Bhadrapada), the remainder 0.77×60=46.00 ghati, remainder 0.00×60=00.00pal, remainder 0.00×60=0.00 vipal were obtained, i.e. 24 Pravistha Bhadrapada, 1889th Shaka Samvat, the 24th fraction had started from 48 ghati, 0pal and 0.00 vipal.

Bhogya Year:- 1944.75+15.31=1960.07 Samvat Decimal will end the 24th part, decimal after digits 0.07×12=0.80 months (Chaitra), remainder 0.8×31=24 Pravisthe (25 Chaitra), remainder 0.00×60=0 Ghati, The digits after the decimal were obtained 0.00×60=0 pal, the remainder 0.0×60=0.000 vipal, that is, on 25 Pravistha Chaitra, 1961st Shaka Samvat, the 25th fraction will start from 0ghati, 0pal and 0 vipal.

Bhukta-Bhogya Table.			
	Bhukta year	Month	Day
AD	1966.70	8.41 (September)	13
Vikrami Samvat	2023.41	4.97 (Bhadrapada)	30
Shaka Samvat	1888.48	5.77 (Bhadrapada)	24
	Bhogya year	Month	Day
AD	2038.29	3.45 (April)	14
Vikrami Samvat	2095.00	0.01 (May)	1
Shaka Samvat	1960.07	0.80 (Chaitra)	25

Ganavarshaadi Bhukt-Bhogya Table.		
	(c) Ganavarsha	(c) Ganavarsha
Bhukta/Bhogya	24.13 victims	341.13 Bhogya
R. P.(Season Change)	0.7	0.93
Mass	0.79	11.21
Entries	24.13	6.30

Samvat Difference Years Table.		
Samvat	Bhukta year	Month
AD	1966.70	8.41 (September)
Vikrami Samvat	2023.41	4.97 (Bhadrapada)
Difference	**56.71 years**	**3.44 (3.44/12=0.29 Years)**
Vikrami Samvat	2023.41	4.97 (Bhadrapada)
Shaka Samvat	1888.48	5.77 (Bhadrapada)
Difference	**134.93 years**	**0.80 (0.80/12=0.07 Years)**
AD	1966.70	8.41 (September)
Shaka Samvat	1888.48	5.77 (Bhadrapada)
Difference	**78.22 years**	**2.64 (20 March)**

Confirmation:- See the above Samvat difference Varshadi table, the difference between AD and Vikrami Samvat is 56.71 Varshadi, whereas in the previous example A-Ganavarsha this difference was 56.78 Varshadi. The difference between the two is 56.78-56.71=0.07 Varshadi, which is the seasonal change from Ayanamsha zero year to the present.

Note, 0.22 Varshadhi keeps decreasing in each cycle, in the 150th Chakra there was a difference of 57 years, in the 151st Chakra this difference became 56.78, currently the 152nd Chakra is going on, in which till now 0.07 Varshadhi has reduced. At the end of the 152nd cycle, 56.56 years will remain. This is the period of one cycle from 21st March to 20th March, which is included in the calendar calculation.

Look at the Samvat difference Varshadi table itself, the difference between Vikrami Samvat and Shaka Samvat is found to be 134.93 Varshadi, whereas in the previous example A-Ganavarsha this difference was 135 years. The difference between the two is 135-134.93= 0.07 Varshadi, which is the difference from Ayanamsha zero year to the present.

Note, the said difference is 0.07 Bhukta Chak Varshadi, Chak Bhogya is 0.93 Varshadi, which is equivalent to 0.15 Varshadi. See the calculation, 0.93×12=11.16 months+2.65=13.81-12=1.81 months, 1.81/12=0.15 years etc. 0.93 the month was made by multiplying it by 12, in this Masadi the month of March 21 was decimalised, the sum was more than 12, It was subtracted, the remainder was divided by 12 and we got 0.15 or 0.22+0.93=1.15chakra, this is more than one chakra, hence by subtracting one we get 0.15.

See the samvat difference varshadi table, the difference between AD and Shaka samvat is found to be 78.22 varshadi, in the previous example A-Ganvarshadi also this difference was 78.22 Varshadi. Since these are sayan years, their difference always remains the same. It has also been written in this regard in the chapter on determining the era.

Hari Om

CHAPTER TWELVE

ONE THE DAY'S SEASON CHANGE BHUKTA AND BHOGYA YEARS ETC.

Seasonal change days are indicative of Bhukta Days, which day of seasonal change is going on at present? How many years have passed since that day and how many more years are left...? to calculate it is being given in detail.

By multiplying the digits after the decimal point in the season change day by 70.56, Bhukta Varshadi is obtained. After subtracting the Bhukta years from 70.56 Varshadi, Bhogya Varshadi is obtained.

By subtracting the Bhukta years from the Ishta years (present day Vikrami, Shaka or AD), the starting time of one day of seasonal change is known and by adding the Bhogya years to the Ishta years, the ending time of one day of seasonal change is known.

Part-1, A.D. pattern (spent year):- In the previous example, the season of the end of Triyuga or the beginning of Kaliyuga. The change was of 316.77 days i.e. the 317th day was going on. Bhukta and Bhogya of 317th day calculate the years. On the day of seasonal change, the figures after decimal were obtained as 0.77×70.56=54.33 years of spent years. These Bhukta Varshadis were subtracted from the Ishtavarshas, 22350-54.33=22295.67 varsha were obtained. The 317th day had started in the said years of 151st Chakra.

0.67×12=8.06 months (September), remainder 0.06×30=1.86 days (2 September), remainder 0.86×24=20.53 hours, remainder 0.53×60=32.03 minutes, remainder 0.03×60= 2.08 seconds were obtained i.e. 151st In the 22296th year of Sayan Chakra, the 317th day started on 2nd September at 20:32 minutes and 2.08 seconds.

Bhogya Varsha:- To find out the end period of 317th day, add 70.56 years to the initial period or subtract the Bhogya year from 70.56 years and add Ishtavarsha to the remainder, 70.56-54.33=16.23 years are obtained. These were added to Ishtavarsha, after 22350+16.23=22366.23 years, the 317th day ended or the 318th day started.

0.23×12=2.73 months (March), remaining 0.73×31=22.72 days (23 March), remaining 0.72×24=17.3 hours, remaining 0.3×60=18.19 minutes, remaining 0.19×60=11.67 seconds were obtained i.e. 151st Sayan Chakra The 317th day ended on March 23 in the 22367th year at 17:18 minutes and 11.67 seconds.

Vikami Pattern (Spent Year):- In the above AD model example, 54.33 Bukta years were obtained, by subtracting the said Bukta Varshadi from the 22349.91 Varshadi (22350-0.09 R.P.) of Nirayan Surya at the end of Triyuga or the beginning of Kaliyuga, the initial period of 317th day will be obtained. And Nirayan Surya on 16.23 Bhogya Varshadi by adding it to the years, the end period of 317th day of seasonal change will be obtained.

Subtracting Bhukta Varshadi from Ishtavarsha, 22349.91-54.33=22295.58 years were obtained. The 317th day had started in the said years of 151st Chakra.

0.58×12=7.01 month (Margashirsha), remaining 0.01×30=0.29 days (1 Margashirsha), remaining 0.29×60=17.36 Ghati, remaining 0.36×60=21.63 pal, remaining 0.63×60=37.56 Vipaladi obtained i.e. 151st Sayan In the 22296th year of Chakra, the 317th day started from 1st entry Margashirsha at 17 Ghati, 21 Pal and 37.56 Vipaladi.

Bhogya Varsha:- To find out the end time of 317th day, by adding 16.23 Bhogya years to Ishtavarsha, 22349.91+16.23=22366.14 years were obtained, after 22367 years, 317th day ended or 318th day started.

0.14×12=1.68 month (Jyeshtha), remaining 0.68×32=21.78 days (22 Jyeshtha), remaining 0.78×60=46.99 Ghati, remaining 0.99×60=59.69 pal, remaining 0.69×60=41.55 Vipaladi obtained i.e. 151st Sayan In the 22367th year of Chakra, the 317th day ended on 22 Jyeshtha at 46 Ghati, 59 Pal and 41.55 Paladi.

Shaka pattern (spent years): - In the above AD pattern example, 54.33 years of spent years were obtained, on subtracting the said spent years from 22349.78 years ((22350-0.22 R.P. (0.09+0.13)) at the end of Triyuga or the beginning of Kaliyuga, it would be 317th. The starting time of the day will be obtained and by adding 16.23 Bhogya Varshadi to Sayan Surya Varshadi, the ending time of - 317th day of season change will be obtained.

Subtracting Bhukta Varshadi from Ishtavarsha, 22349.78-54.33=22295.45 years were obtained. The 317th day had started in the said years of 151st Chakra.

0.45×12=5.42 months (Bhadrapada), remainder 0.42×30=12.92 days (13Bhadrapada), remainder 0.92×60=55.05 Ghati, remainder 0.05×60=2.76 pal, remainder 0.76×60=45.38 Vipaladi obtained i.e. 151st Sayan Chakra. In the 22296th year of 13th entry Bhadrapada, the 317th day started with 55 Ghati, 2 Pal and 45.38 Vipaladi.

Bhogya Varsha:- To find out the end time of 317th day, by adding 16.23 Bhogya years to Ishtavarsha, 22349.78+16.23=22366.01 years were obtained, after 22367th year, 317th day ended or 318th day started.

0.01×12=0.09 month (Chaitra), remainder 0.09×32=2.63 days (3 Chaitra), remainder 0.63×60=37.99 Ghati, remainder 0.99×60=59.5 pal, remainder 0.5×60=30.19 Vipaladi obtained i.e. 151st Sayan In the 22367th year of Chakra, 3 chaitra ended on the 317th day at 37 Ghati, 59 Pal and 30.19 Paladi.

Note, the Vikami Samvat Pattern Bhukta month was 7.01 and the Bhogya month was 1.68 and the Shaka Samvat Pattern Bhukta month was 5.42 and the Bhogya month was 0.09. If we differentiate the month of Bhukta from Bhukta or Bhogya month from Bhogya, then the Bhogya month of Part-2 is only 1.59. Like Bhukta 7.01-Bhukta 5.42=1.59 months, like Bhogya 1.68-Bhogya 0.09=1.59 months. The first part Bhukta of the Chakra was 10.41 months, the second part Bhogya of the Chakra was 1.59 months, the sum of both is 12 months, the above calculation is also confirmed.

Samvat Bhukta-Bhogya Table			
	Bhukta Years	Month	Day
AD pattern	22295.67	8.06 (September)	2
Vikrami pattern	22295.58	7.01 (Margashirsha)	1
Shaka pattern	22295.45	5.42 (Bhadrapada)	13
	Bhogya Years	Month	Day
AD pattern	22366.23	2.73 (March)	23
Vikrami pattern	22366.14	1.68 (Jyestha)	22
Shaka pattern	22366.01	0.09 (Chaitra)	3

Season difference table.		
	Bhukta year	Month
AD pattern	22295.67	8.06 (September)
Vikrami pattern	22295.58	7.01 (March)
Season difference	0.09	1.05 (1.05/12=0.09)
Vikrami pattern	22295.58	7.01 (Margashirsha)
Shaka pattern	22295.45	5.42 (Bhadrapada)
Season difference	0.13	1.59 (1.59/12=0.13)
AD pattern	22295.67	8.06 (September)
Shaka pattern	22295.45	5.42 (Bhadrapada)
Season difference	0.22	2.64 (2.64/12=0.22)

Ganavarshaadi Bhukt Bhogya Table.		
	(a) Ganavarsha	(b) Ganavarsha
Bhukta/Bhogya	316.77 Bhukta	48.49 Bhogya
S.C. Varsadi	0.87 or 0.09	0.13
Month	10.41	1.59
Pravistha	12.39	18.05

Confirm the calculations yourself by looking at the seasonal difference table above. The change of season till the end of Dwaparayuga is 0.09 years and the change of season from the beginning of Kali to the end of Ayanamsha Shunya year is 0.13 years.

BC (Years passed):- 3101+54.33=3155.33 BC The 317th day started. 0.33×12=3.94 months (April), remainder 0.94×30=28.14 days (April 29), remainder 0.14×24=3.47 hours, remainder 0.47×60=27.97 minutes, remainder 0.97×60=57.92 seconds were obtained i.e. 3156 BC. The 317th day started on April 29 at 3:27 minutes and 57.92 seconds.

BC (Bhogya year):- 3101-16.23=3084.77 BC ended on the 317th day. 0.77×12=9.27 months (October), remaining 0.27×31=8.28 days (9 October), remaining 0.28×24=6.7 hours, remaining 0.7×60=41.81 minutes, remaining 0.81×60=48.33 seconds were obtained i.e. 3085 BC 9 The 317th day ended on October 6 at 6:41 minutes and 48.33 seconds.

Before Vikami (Years passed):- 3044.09 years+54.43=3098.42 Vikrami Samvat Purva started on the 317th day. Decimal figures 0.42×12=4.99 months (Bhadrapada), Decimal figures 0.99×30=29.71 entries (30 Bhadrapada), remainder 0.71×60=42.64Ghati, remainder 0.64×60=38.37 Pal, remainder 0.37×60=22.45 Vipal was received i.e. 317th day started from 42 Ghati, 38 Pal and 22.45 Vipal on 30 Bhadrapada of 3099th Before Vikrami Samvat.

Before Vikami (Bhogya Year):- 3044.09-16.23=3027.86 Vikrami Samvat Purva 317th day ended. Decimal figures 0.86×12=10.32 months (Phalgun), Decimal figures 0.32×30=9.58 entries (10 Phalguna), remainder 0.58×60=34.69 Ghati, remainder 0.69×60=41.54 Pal, remainder 0.54×60=32.31 Vipal was received i.e. 317th day ended in 3028th Vikrami Samvat Purva, 10th entry of Phalgun month in 34 Ghati, 41 Pal and 32.31 Vipaladi.

Before Shaka (Spent Year):- 3179.22+54.43=3233.55 Shaka Samvat Purva started on the 317th day. Decimal figures 0.55×12=6.58 months (Ashvin), Decimal figures 0.58×30=17.5 entries (18 Ashvins), remainder 0.5×60=29.96 Ghatis, remainder 0.96×60=57.33 Pal, remainder 0.33×60=19.96 Vipal was received i.e. 317th day started from 29 Ghati, 57 Pal and 19.96 Vipal on 18th Ashwin month of 3234th Shaka Samvat.

Before Shaka (Bhogya Year):- 3179.22-16.23=3162.99 Shaka Samvat Purva 317th day ended. Post decimal figures 0.99×12=11.91 months (Phalgun), Post decimal figures 0.91×30=27.37 entries (28 Phalguna), remainder 0.37×60=22.01 Ghati, remainder 0.01×60= 0.5 pal, remainder 0.5×60=29.82 Vipals were received i.e. 3163rd before Shaka Samvat, on 28th Phalgun month, 22 Ghati, 0 Pal and 29.82 Vipaladi in 317th day ended.

Before Samvat Bhukta-Bhogya Table.			
	Spent year	Month	Day
B.C	3155.33	3.94 (April)	29
Before Vikrami	3233.55	4.99 (Bhadrapada)	30
Before Shaka	3098.42	6.58 (Ashwin)	18
	Bhogya year	Month	Day
B.C	3084.77	9.27 (October)	9
Before Vikrami	3027.86	10.32 (Phalgun)	10
Before Shaka	3162.99	11.91 (Phalgun)	28

Season difference table.		
Samvat	Bhukta years	Months
AD	3155.33	3.94 (April)
Vikrami Samvat	3098.42	4.99 (Bhadrapada)
Difference	56.91 years	1.05 (1.05/12=0.09 years)
Vikrami Samvat	3098.42	4.99 (Bhadrapada)
Shaka Samvat	3233.55	6.58 (Ashwin)
Difference	135.13 years	1.59 (1.59/12=0.13)
AD	3155.33	3.94 (April)
Shaka Samvat	3233.55	6.58 (Ashwin)
Difference	78.22 Year	2.64 (20 March)

Part-2 Ayanamsh Shunyakaal (Bhuktavarsha):- Example is of Ayanamsh Shunyakaal, there the seasonal change is also zero, the seasonal change of the said period of 3421 years was 48.49 days. Starting day 48 and ending day 0.49 of the said day were multiplied by 70.56 years separately, 48×70.56=3386.68 years, added these years in Ishtavarsha, 22350+3386.68=25736.68 years were obtained, 49th in 25736.68 years of 151st Chakra The day had started. 0.68×12=8.21 months (September), remaining 0.21×30=6.36 days (7 September), remaining 0.36×24=8.59 hours, remaining 0.59×60=35.25 minutes, remaining 0.25×60=14.75 seconds were obtained i.e. 151st Sayan Chakra The 48th day started on 7th September in the year 25737 at 8:35 minutes and 14.75 seconds.

Bhogya year:- To find out the end period of 0.49 days out of 48.49 days of seasonal change, 0.49 was multiplied by 70.56 years, 0.49×70.56=34.32 Bhogya years, 25736.68+34.32=25771 years were obtained, i.e. at the end of 151st Sayan Chakra, 25771 years were obtained. The 48.49th seasonal change day of the year ended on March 21 at 00:00.

AD (Spent Year):- Season change: From the spent years of 48 days, the middle period (3101) from the beginning of Kaliyuga to the beginning of AD has to be subtracted, 3386.68-3101=285.68 are obtained, Decimal figures 0.68×12=8.21 months (September), Decimal figures 0.21×30=6.36 days (September 7), remainder 0.36×24=8.59 hours, remainder 0.59×60=35.25 minutes, remainder 0.25×60=14.75 seconds were obtained i.e. the 48th day started from 8:35 AM and 14.75 seconds on 7th September in the 286th year of 151st Sayan Chakra.

Bhogya year:- By adding 0.49 days of Bhogya year and 21st March (0.22) year decimal to the above mentioned starting period of 285.68 years, the end period of seasonal change is obtained on 48.49th day in AD. The spent year ended on the 48.49th day of initial period 285.68+34.54 (34.32+0.22)=320.22 AD.

Part-3. Spent year of AD:- In the above example, the change of season of 22 December 2023 AD was found to be 24.13 days i.e. the 25th day was going on. Bhukta and Bhogya of the 25th day calculate the years. Multiplying the decimal number in the date of seasonal change by 70.56 years, we get 0.13×70.56 = 9.41 spent years.

By subtracting the spent years from the Ishta years, the starting period of the 25th day is obtained, the 25th day started in the Ishta years 2022.97-9.41=2013.56.

0.56×12=6.75 months (July), remaining 0.75×31=23.28 days (24th July), remaining 0.28×24= 6.84 hours, remaining 0.84×60=50.21 minutes, remaining 0.21×60=12.6 seconds etc., i.e. 24 The 25th day started at 6:50 minutes and 12.60 seconds on July 2014.

Bhogya Varsha:- To find the end period of 25th day, the end period is known by adding 70.56 years to the initial period or by subtracting the Bhukta from 70.56 years and adding the remainder to the Ishta years.

70.56-9.41=61.15 years were obtained, adding these to the auspicious years, it will end on 25th day after 2022.97+61.15=2084.12 years.

0.12×12=1.42 months (February), remaining 0.42×28=11.82 days (12 February), remaining 0.82×24=19.72 hours, remaining 0.72×60=43.37 minutes, remaining 0.37×60=22.18 seconds etc., obtained on 12 February The 25th day will end on 2085 AD at 19:43 minutes and 22.18 seconds.

Vikrami Samvat Bhukt Varsh:- The above example is of 8th Paush Vishnu 2080, by subtracting the above 9.41 Bhukt Varsh from Ishtavarsh 2079.69 years, the initial period of 25th day will be obtained, 2079.69-9.41=2070.28 years, Shravan of 2071st Vikrami Samvat is 10 entries, 23 Ghati, 34 Pal and the 25th day started at 10.95 Vipal.

Bhogya Varsha:- 61.15 Bhogya Varsha, added to these Ishtavarshas, 2079.69-61.15= 2140.83 Varsha, 2141st Vikrami Samvat will end on the 25th day after Magh 30 Pravisthe, 31 Ghati, 31 Pal and 1.09 Vipal.

Shaka Samvat Bhukta year:- The above example is of 1st Paush Shaka 1945 year, by subtracting the above 9.41 Bhukta year from Ishtavarsha 1944.75 years, the starting period of 25th day will be obtained, 1944.75-9.41=1935.34 year, Shravan 4 entries of 1936th Shaka Samvat, 17 Ghati, The 25th day started at 5 Pal and 31.50 Vipal.

Bhogya Varsha:- 61.15 Bhogya Varsha, added to these Ishtavarshas, 1944.75+61.15= 2005.90 Varsha, 2006th Shaka Samvat will end on the 25th day after Magh 24 Pravisthe, 18 Ghati, 40 Pal and 53.53 Vipal.

Samvat Bhukta-Bhogya Table.			
	Bhukta year	Month	Day
AD	2013.56	6.75 (July)	24
Vikrami Samvat	2070.28	3.31 (Shravan)	10
Shaka Samvat	1935.34	4.11 (Shravan)	4
	Bhogya year	Month	Day
AD	2084.12	1.42 (February)	12
Vikrami Samvat	2140.83	9.98 (Magh)	30
Shaka Samvat	2005.90	10.78 (Magh)	24

Season difference table.		
Samvat	Bhukta years	Month
AD	2013.56	6.75 (July)
Vikrami Samvat	2070.28	3.31 (Shravan)
Difference	56.71 years	3.44 (3.44/12=0.29 Varshadi)
Vikrami Samvat	2070.28	3.31 (Shravan)
Shaka Samvat	1935.34	4.11 (Shravan)
Difference	134.93 years	0.79 (0.79/12=0.07 Varshadi)
AD	2013.56	6.75 (July)
Shaka Samvat	1935.34	4.11 (Shravan)
Difference	78.22 years	2.64.(20 March)

Ganavarshaadi Bhukta-Bhogya Table.		
	(c) Ganavarsha	(c) Ganavarsha
Bhukta/Bhogya	24.13 Bhukta	341.12 Bhogya
R P Varsadi	0.07	0.93
Mass	0.79	11.21
Entries	24.13	6.30

Hari Om

CHAPTER THIRTEEN

BHUKT-BHOGYA VARSHADI OF A ZODIAC SIGN OR MONTH

In the above section, the calculation of one day's Bhukta and Bhogya has been done, here the calculation of one month's Bhukta and Bhogya is being given in detail. In the annual movement, the Sun completes one degree in approximately one day and one degree in one month. Whereas in Ayana Chakra movement, the Sun completes one day in 70.56 years and completes one month in 2147.58 years.

Below is the table of seasonal changes of Bhukt Bhogya of Kaliyugarambh and Ayanamsh Shunyavarsha. On the basis of the table, the Bhukt Bhogya of the month is calculated.

Ganavarshaadi Bhukta-Bhogya table.		
	(a) Ganavarsha	(b) Ganavarsha
Bhukta/Bhogya	316.77 Bhokta	48.49 Bhogya
R P Varsadi	0.87 or 0.09	0.13
Mass	10.41	1.59
Pravistha	12.39	18.05

Ishtavarsha table.			
	Sayan	Nirayan	Sayan
Bhukta	22350.00	22349.91	22349.78
Bhogya	3101.00	3044.09	3179.22

Rashi (Sign) Bhukta-Bhogya Varshadi, Method-1:- Bhukta Varshadi is obtained by multiplying the Bhukta month of seasonal change with the decimal number followed by the twelfth part of Chakra years 2147.58 (25771/12), by subtracting the Bhukta Varshdi from Ishtavarsha, month is obtained. Initial period of is obtained. By subtracting Bhukta Varshadi from 2147.58 Varshadi, Bhogya Varshadi is obtained. By adding Bhogya Varshadi to Ishtavarsha, the end period of month or zodiac is obtained.

Rashi Bhukta-Bhogya Varshadi, Method-2:- Bhukta Varshadi is obtained by multiplying the Bhukta entry decimal by 70.56. By subtracting Bhukta Varshadi from Ishtavarsha, the initial period of the month is obtained. In the same manner, by multiplying the Bhogya entry decimal by 70.56, Bhogya Varshadi is obtained, by adding Bhogya Varshadi to Ishtavarsha, the end period of the month is obtained.

In Bhukta and Bhogya Varshadi, by multiplying the digits after the decimal by 12, the month of January etc. is obtained, by multiplying the remainder with the days of the respective January, Baishakhadi and Chaitradi months, the days are obtained, the remainder is obtained by multiplying the number by 24 or 60. By multiplying, we get hours or Ghati, by multiplying the remainder by 60, we get minutes or pals and by multiplying the remainder by 60, we get seconds or vipal.

Example:- At the time of end of Triyuga or beginning of Kaliyuga, Bhukta was found to be 10.41 mas decimal and Bhogya was 1.59 mas decimal and Bhuk entry was found to be 12.39 and Bhogya entry was 18.05.

Method 1:- Digits after decimal in month decimal 0.41×(25771/12)=874.17 Bhukta Varshadi, subtracted Bhukta Varshdi from Ishtavarsha, 22350-874.17=21475.83 Bhukta Varshdi, initial period of Aquarius was obtained. Bhogya Varshadi, digits after decimal 0.59×(25771/12)=1273.42 Bhogya Varshadi, adding Bhogya Varshadi in Ishtavarsha, 22350+1273.42=23623.42, then the end period of Aquarius was obtained.

Method 2 (Bhukta Varshadi):- Bhukta Varshadi 12.39×70.56=874.17 Bhukta Varshadi, subtracted Bhukta Varshadi from Ishtavarsha,

22350-874.17=21475.83 Bhukta Varsha, the entry period of Aquarius was obtained. 0.83×12=9.99 Month (October), 0.99×31=30.99 Days, it had been 874.17 years since the Sayan Sun entered Aquarius, or the Sayan Sun, in the 21476th year of the 151st Chakra at 0:00 PM on 31st October. Entered Aquarius in minutes and 0.00 seconds.

Bhogya Varshadi:- Bhogya entry 18.05×70.56=1273.42 Bhogya Varshadi, adding Bhogya Varshadi in Ishtavarsha, 22350+1273.42=23623.42, then the end period of Aquarius was obtained.

Decimal numbers 0.42×12=4.99 Month (May), 0.99×31=30.99 Days, Sayan Sun has yet to remain in Aquarius for 1273.42 years, or Sayan Sun has to remain in Aquarius in the 22624th year of the 151st Chakra at 31 May, 00 hrs, The position remained in Aquarius for 0 minutes, that is, for the next 1273.42 years Baisakhi was falling in autumn only.

Bhukta calculations according to Vikrami pattern:- End of Dwapara Yuga Nirayana Ishtavarsha 22349.91-874.17=21475.75 Bhuktavarsha, In the 21476th Nirayana Samvat, on Paush 29 Pravisthe, the Sayan Sun entered Aquarius at 26 Ghati, 1 Pal and 32.35 Vipal.

Bhogya calculation:- Dwaparayug end period Nirayan Ishtavarsha 22349.91+1273.42= 23623.33 Bhogyavarsha, in 23624th Nirayan Samvat, on Shravan 29 Pravisht, the Sayan Sun entered Pisces at 26 Ghati, 1 Pal and 32.35 Vipal, with this now for the next 4295.17 years (2 months). Till then, that is, from Pisces to Aries, there will be spring season.

Bhukta calculations according to Shaka samvat model:- End of Dwapara Yuga Sayan Ishta 22349.78-874.17=21475.61 Bhuktavarsha, 21476th Sayan Samvat, Kartik 11 Pravisthe, Sayan Sun entered Aquarius at 38 Ghati, 42 Pal and 34.84 vipals.

Bhogya calculation:- Dwaparayuga end period Nirayan Ishtavarsha 22349.78+1273.42= 23623.20 Bhogyavarsha, in 23624th Sayan Samvat, on Jyeshtha 11 Pravistha, Sayan Sun entered Pisces at 0 Ghati, 0 Pal and 0.0 Vipal.

Sign entry and exit table.			
Entry time	Year	Month	Day
Sayan Years	21476	October	31
Nirayan Years	21476	Paush	29
Sayan Years	21476	Kartika	11
Exit time	Year	Month	Day
Sayan Years	23624	May	31
Nirayan Years	23624	Sravan	29
Sayan Years	23624	Jyestha	11

Season difference table.		
Samvat	Bhukta Years	Month
Sayan year	21475.83	10.00 (October)
Nirayan year	21475.75	8.95 (Poush)
Difference	0.09 years	1.05 (1.05/12=0.9 Years)
Nirayan year	21475.75	8.95 (Poush)
Sayan year	21475.61	7.35 (Kartik)
Difference	0.13 years	1.59 (1.59/12=0.13 Years)
Sayan year	21475.83	10.00 (October)
Sayan year	21475.61	7.35 (Kartik)
Difference	0.22 years	2.65 (21 March)

BC (Bhukta Varshadi):- By adding the Bhukta years to 3101, the entry time of the zodiac sign in BC and subtracting the Bhogya years from 3101, the end time of the zodiac position can be found in BC. Note, the Ishtavarsha or Ganavarsha of Dwaparayuga is 22350, that is, Dwaparayuga ended here, after which Kaliyuga started, which is 3101 years till the beginning of AD. Therefore, in 3101 years, one has to add and subtract one's Bhukta-Bhogya.

3101+874.17=3975.17 years, 0.17×12=1.99 Masadi (February), 0.99×28=27.99 days, 0.99×24=24 hours, 0.00×60=00.00 minutes, 0.00×60=00.00 seconds, Sayan Sun entered Aquarius. Entered in 3976 BC on 28th February, 00:00 minutes and 00.00 seconds.

BC (Bhogya Varshadi):- By subtracting the Bhogya years from 3101, the end time of the zodiac position can be found in BC. 3101-1273.42=1827.58 years, decimal 0.58×12=6.99 masadi (July), 0.99×30=30.99 days, 0.99×24=24.00 hrs., 0.00×60=00.00 minutes, 0.00×60= 00.00 seconds, Sayan Sun remained in Aquarius till 31st July, 1828 BC, at 24:00, 00 minutes and 00.00 seconds.

Before Vikrami (Bhukta Varshadi):- By adding the years spent before the end of the year to 3044.09, the amount before the end of the year, entry period and benefits will be obtained. By subtracting the years from 3044.09, the end period of the zodiac position can be determined in advance. Note, the Ishtavarsha or Ganavarsha of Dwaparayuga is 22349.91, that is, Dwaparayuga ended here, after which Kaliyuga started, which is 3044.09 years till the beginning of Vikrami Samvat. Therefore, in 3044.09 years, one has to add or subtract one's Bhukta-Bhogya.

3044.09+874.17=3918.25 years, 0.25×12=3.05 masadi (Shravan), 0.05×30=1.57 Parvishte, 0.57×60=33.97 ghati, 0.97×60=58.46 pal, 0.46×60=27.66 vipaladhi, Sayan surya enter Aquarius in before 3919 Vikrami Samvat , 2 entries were made in Shravan month, 33 Ghati, 58 Pal and 27.66 Vipaladi.

Before Vikrami (Bhogya Varshadi):- By subtracting the Bhogya years from 3044.09, the end period of the zodiac position can be found in Vikami Purva. 3044.09-1273.42=1770.67 years, 0.67×12=8.05 masadi (pausha), decimal 0.05×30=1.57 entries, decimal 0.57×60=33.97 ghati, decimal 0.97×60=58.46 pal, 0.46×60=27.66 Vipaladi, Sayan Sun remained in Aquarius sign till 1771 Vikami Samvat Purva, 2nd entry Paush month, 33 Ghati, 58 Pal and 27.66 Vipaladi.

Before Shaka (Bhukta Varshadi):- By adding the Bhukta years to 3179.22, the Sign before Shaka is the entry period and Bhogya years. By subtracting 3179.22, the end time of zodiac position can be determined in advance. Note, the Ishtavarsha or Ganavarsha of Dwaparyug is 22349.78. That is, Dwaparayuga ended here, after which Kaliyuga started, which is 3179.22 years till the beginning of Shaka Samvat. Therefore, in 3179.22 years, one has to add or subtract one's Bhukta-Bhogya.

3179.22+874.17=4053.39 years, 0.39×12=4.65 Masadi (Shravan), 0.65×31=20 Parivishte, 0.0×60=00.00 Ghati, 0.00×60=00.00 Paladi, 0.00×60=00.00 Vipaladi, Sayan Sun entered Aquarius. In 4054 Shaka Samvat ago, 21 entries were made in Shravan month, 0 Ghati, 0 Pal and 0.0 Vipaladi.

Before Shaka (Bhogya Varshadi):- By subtracting the Bhogya years from 3179.22, the end period of the zodiac position can be found in Shaka Before. 3179.22-1273.42=1905.80 years, 0.8×12=9.65 Masadi (Paush), Decimal digits 0.65×30=19.35 entries, Decimal digits 0.35×60= 21.29 Ghati, Decimal digits 0.29×60=17.42 Paladi, 0.42×60=25.17 Vipaladi, Sayan Sun remained in Aquarius sign till 1906 Shaka Samvat 20 Pravisht

Paush month, 21 Ghati, 17 Pal and 25.17 Vipaladi.

Sign entry and exit table.			
Entry time	Year	Month	Day
B.C.	3976	February	28
Before Vikrami	3919	Shravan	2
Before Shaka	4054	Shravan	21
Exit time	Year	Month	Day
B.C.	1828	July	31
Before Vikrami	1771	Pausha	2
Before Shaka	1906	Pausha	20

Season difference table.		
Samvat	Bhukta years	Months
BC	3975.17	2.0..(March)
Before Vikrami	3918.25	3.05 (Shravan)
Difference	56.91 years	1.05 (1.05/12=0.09)
Before Vikrami	3918.25	3.05 (Shravan)
Before Shaka	4053.39	4.65 (Shravan)
Difference	135.13 years	1.59 (1.59/12=0.13)
BC	3975.17	2.0..(March)
Before Shaka	4053.39	4.65 (Shravan)
Difference	78.22 years	2.64 (20 March)

Example, Part-3:- On 22nd December 2023, see in the desired year table, Bhukta entry 24.13 and Bhogya entry 6.30 were known.

Ganavarshaadi Bhukta-Bhogya Table.		
	(c) Ganavarsha	(c) Ganavarsha
Bhukta/Bhogya	24.13 Bhukta	341.12 Bhogya
R P Varsadi	0.07	0.93
Month	0.79	11.21
Entries	24.13	6.30

Ishtavarsha table.			
	Sayan Isht.	Nirayan Isht.	Sayan Isht.
Bhukta	2022.97	2079.69	1944.75
Bhogya	23748.03	23691.31	23826.25
Ganavarsha	1702.75	1702.69	1702.75

AD, Method 2 (Bhukta Varshadi):- Bhukta entries 24.13×70.56=1702.75 Bhukta Varshadi, Bhukta from Ishtavarsha Subtracting Varshadi, 2022.97-1702.75=320.22 years, entry period of Sayan Aries was obtained. 0.22×12=2.65 Masadi (March), 0.22×31=20 Days, it has been 1702.75 years since the Sayan Sun entered Aries, or the Sayan Sun entered the zodiac sign Aries on March 21 at 00:00 AM in the 321st year of the 152nd Chakra. Had entered Aries on the minute.

Bhogya Varshadi:- Bhogya entry 6.3×70.56=444.83 years, Bhogya Varshadi added in Ishtavarsha, Ishtavarsha 2022.97+444.83=2467.8 years, the end period of Sayan Aries was obtained. 0.8×12=9.65 Masadi (October), 0.65×31=20.00 Dinadi, 0.00×24=00.00 Hour, 0.00×60=0.0 Minute, 0.00×60=00.00 Second, Sayan Sun still has to remain in Aries for 444.83 years , or Sayan, in the 2468th year of the 152nd cycle, the Sun will remain in Aries till 21st October, 00:00, 00.00 seconds, that is, for the next 444.83 years, Baisakhi will continue to fall in the spring season, after which Vaisakhi will start in the summer season.

Vikrami Samvat, Bhukta Varshadi:- Bhukta entry 2079.69-377 years=1702.69 Bhukta Varshadi, Bhukta years etc. from desired years Subtracted, 2079.69-1702.69=377 years, entry period of Sayan Aries was obtained. 0.0×12=0.0 Masadi (Chaitra), 0.0×31=30 Dinadi, It has been 1702.69 years since the Sayan Sun entered Aries, or the Sayan Sun entered the 378th year of the 152nd Chakra on 31 Chaitra at 00 Gahti, 00 pal. But had entered Aries. Refer to the previous chapter regarding Ganavarsha.

Bhogya Varshadi:- Bhogya entry 6.3×70.56=444.83 years+0.07=444.90 Bhogya years, Bhogya Varshadi was added to Ishtavarsha, 2079.69+444.90 = 2524.58 years, the end period of Sayan Aries was obtained. 0.58×12=7 Masadi (Kartik), 0.00×31=30 Dinadi, 0.00×24=00.00 Ghati, 0.00×60=00.00 Paladi, 0.00×60-00.00 Vipaladi, Sayan Sun still has 444.90 years to stay in Aries , or Sayan, in the 2525th year of the 152nd cycle, the Sun will remain in Aries till 31st Kartik, 00Ghati, 00Pal and 00.00 Vipaladi.

Shaka Samvat, Bhukta Varshadi:- Bhukta Pravishthe 1944.75-242.00=1702.75 Bhukta Varshadi, subtracted Bhukta Varshadi from Ishtavarsha, Ishtavarsha 1944.75-1702.75= 242.00 year, entry period of Sayan Aries was obtained. 0.0×12=0.0 Masadi (Phalgun), 0.0×31=30 Dinadi, it has been 1702.75 years since the Sayan Sun entered Aries, or the Sayan Sun entered the 243rd year of the 152nd Chakra on 31 Phalguna at 00 Ghati, 00 Pal. Had entered Aries.

Bhogya Varshadi:- 444.83 Bhogya Varsha, Bhogya Varshadi was added to Ishtavarsha, 1944.75+444.83=2389.58 years, the end period of Sayan Aries was obtained. 0.58×12=7 Masadi (Ashwin), 0.00×31=30 Dinadi, 0.0×24=0 Ghati, 0.00×60=00.00 Paladi, 0.00×60-00.00 Vipaladi, Sayan Sun has 444.83 more years to remain in Aries. Or, in the 2390th year of the 152nd cycle of the Sayan Sun, its position will remain in Aries till 31 Pravisht Ashwin, 00 Ghati, 00 Pal and 00.00 Vipaladi.

Sign entry and exit table.			
entry time	Year	Mass	Day
AD	320.22	March	21
Vikrami Samvat	377.00	Chaitra	31
Shaka Samvat	242.00	Falgun	31
Exit time	Year	Mass	Day
AD	2467.80	October	21
Vikrami Samvat	2524.58	Kartika	31
Shaka Samvat	2389.58	Ashwin	31

Bhukta season difference table.		
Samvat	Bhukta Years	Month
AD	320.22	2.65 (March)
Vikrami Samvat	377.00	12.00 (Chaitra)
Difference	56.78 years	2.65 (21 March)
Vikrami Samvat	377.00	12.00 (Chaitra)
Shaka Samvat	242.00	12.00 (Phalgun)
Difference	135.00 years	0.00 zero seasonal change
AD	320.22	2.65 (March)
Shaka Samvat	242.00	12.00 (Phalgun)
Difference	78.22 years	2.65 (21 March)

Bhogya season difference table.		
Samvat	Bhukta Years	Month
AD	2467.80	9.65 (October)
Vikrami Samvat	2524.58	7.00 (Karthik)
Difference	56.78 years	2.65 (21 March)
Vikrami Samvat	2524.58	7.00 (Karthik)
Shaka Samvat	2389.58	7.00 (Ashwin)
Difference	135.00 years	0.00 zero seasonal change
AD	2467.80	9.65 (October)
Shaka Samvat	2389.58	7.00 (Ashwin)
Difference	78.22 years	2.65 (21 March)

The above Bhukta-Bhogya table confirms the starting time and ending time of a zodiac sign. During Ayanamsh Zerotime, the said Samvat had enjoyed 320.22, 377, and 242 years respectively. If Bhukta is subtracted from Bhogya years then 2147.58 years of a Rashi confirms the above calculation. Like AD Bhogya 2467.80-320.22=2147.58 Varshadi, understand in the same way further also.

Hari Om

CHAPTER FOURTEEN

CHAKRA'S BHUKTA AND BHOGYA YEARS

Calculation method:- Multiplying the day of seasonal change by Chakra and dividing it by the days of Nirayan Surya year, Bhukta Varshadi is obtained. This is also the reverse calculation method of calculating Ganavarsha from the days of seasonal change. By subtracting the Bhukta year decimal from the Ishtavarsha, the initial period of Chakra is obtained in solar years, hence, add 0.22 (21st March) year decimal in it and make Sayan. In the initial period, the month decimal is obtained by multiplying the digit after the decimal by 12, the day decimal is obtained by multiplying the digit after the decimal by the total number of days of the respective month, the hour decimal is obtained by multiplying the digit after the decimal by 24 and the digit after the decimal is obtained by multiplying the digit after the decimal by 24. Minute decimals are obtained by multiplying by 60.

Bhogya Varshadi is obtained by multiplying the days of seasonal change by Chakra and dividing it by the days of the Nirayan Surya year. By adding Bhogya year decimal to Ishtavarsha, the end period of Chakra is obtained in Sayan years, hence make Sayan by including 0.22 (21st March) year decimal in it. Multiplying the digit after the decimal by 12 gives the month decimal, multiplying the digit after the decimal by the total number of days of the respective month gives the day decimal, multiplying the digit after the decimal by 24 gives the hour decimal and multiplying the digit after the decimal by 60. By multiplying, minute decimals are obtained.

Ishtavarsha table.			
	Sayan Isht.	**Nirayan Isht.**	**Sayan Isht.**
Bhukta	22350.00	22349.91	22349.78
Bhogya	3421.00	3421.09	3421.22

AD Pattern, Bhukta calculation:- End of Triyug or beginning of Kaliyuga period, Bhukt season change date was found to be 316.77 and Bhogya season change date was found to be 48.49. 316.77×25771/365.256363=22350 Bhukta years, by subtracting these years from Ishtavarsha 22350, zero was obtained, adding 0.22 to the zero years and made it sayan. 22350-22350=0+0.22=0.22 Sayan year decimal, 151st cycle started on 21 March.

Bhogya calculation:- 48.49×25771/365.256363=3421 By adding Bhogya Varshadi, Bhogya Varshadi in Ishtavarsha, the end of 151st Chakra is obtained. 22350+3421=25771+0.22= 25771.22 sayan years were obtained. From these years, 25451 years (22350+3101) were subtracted, 25771.22-25451=320.22 years decimal, 0.22×12=2.65 Masadi (March), 0.22×31=20 Dinadi, 151st Chakra completed in the beginning of 21st March in the year 321 AD. or Sayan The Sun entered Aries at 00:00 PM on March 20 in the 321st year of the 152nd Chakra. Note, this is also Ayanamsha Zero Time (21 March 321 AD).

According to Vikrami Samvat Pattern Bhukta calculation:- At the end of Triyuga or Kaliyuga period, Bhukta 22349.91 Varshadi and Bhogya were found to be 3421.09 Varshadi.

316.77×25771/365.256363=22350 Bhukta-0.09RP=22349.91 Nirayan Varshadi, on subtracting these years from Ishtavarsha, 22349.91-22349.91=0 year was obtained, zero, the 151st Chakra started in the zero period of the first entry of Baishakh month.

Bhogya calculation:- 25771-22349.91= 3421.09 By adding Bhogya Varshadi, Bhogya Varshadi to Ishtavarsha, the end of 151st Chakra is obtained. 22349.91+3421.09= 25771 Nirayan years were obtained. From these years, 25394 years (22349.91+3044.09) were subtracted,

25771-25394= 377 years decimal, 0.0×12=0.00 Masadi (Baishakh), 0.0×30= 00 Dinadi, 151st in the initial period of 1 entry in the 378th year of Vikrami Samvat. The cycle was completed or the Nirayan Sun had entered Aries at 00 Ghati, 00 Paladi on 0 Pravisthe Baishakh month in the 378th year of the 152nd Chakra. Note, this is also the last 377 years of Ayanamsha Shunyakaal.

Shaka Samvat Pattern Bhukta Calculation:- Bhogya was found to be 3421.22 Varshadi. The end of Triyuga or the beginning of Kali Yuga, the Bhukta is 22349.78 years old.

316.77×25771/365.256363=22350-0.22RP=22349.78 Sayan Varshadi, on subtracting these years from Ishtavarsha, 22349.78-22349.78=0 year was obtained, zero. The 151st Chakra started in the zero period of the first entry of Chaitra month.

Bhogya calculation:- 25771-22349.78= 3421.22 By adding Bhogya Varshadi, Bhogya Varshadi to Ishtavarsha, the end of 151st Chakra is obtained. 22349.78+3421.22= 25771 sayan years were obtained. From these years, 25529 years (22349.78+3179.22) were subtracted, 25771-25529=242 years decimal, 0.0×12=0.00 Masadi (Chaitra), 0.0×30=00 Dinadi, 151st in the initial period of 1 entry in the 243rd year of Shaka Samvat. Chakra completed or Sayan Sun entered Aries at 00 Ghati, 00 Paladi on 0 Pravisthe Chaitra month in 243rd year of 152nd Chakra. Was. Note, this is also the last 242 years of Ayanamsha Shunyakaal. , Starting and ending time table of 151st cycle.

Starting and ending time table of 151st cycle.		
	Initial period	Exit period
AD Pattern	25451 BC, 21 March	320.22 AD 21 March
Vikrami Pattern	25394 before Nirayan	377 Vikrami 1 Baisakha
Shaka Pattern	25529 before Sayan	242 Shaka 1 Chaitra

Example, Part-3:- Bhukta season change day of 22 December 2023 AD was found to be 24.13 and Bhogya season change day was found to be 341.12.

Ishtavarsha table.			
	Sayan Isht.	Nirayan Isht.	Sayan Isht.
Bhukta	2022.97	2079.69	1944.75
Bhogya	23748.03	23691.31	23826.25
Bhukta Ganavarsha	1702.75	1702.69	1702.75
Bhogya Ganavarsha	24068.25	24068.31	24068.25

Chakra Bhukta Year Calculation A.D.:- 24.13×25771/ 365.256363=1702.75 Bhukta Varshadi, 152nd Chakra started 1702.75 years ago or by subtracting Bhukta years from Ishtavarsha, the starting period of 152nd Chakra is obtained, 2022.97-1702.75=320.22 years. The 152nd Chakra started on 21 March 321 AD.

Chakra Bhogya Varsha Calculation:- By adding 341.12×25771/ 365.256363=24068.25 Bhogya Varshadi to the current Ishtavarsha, the completion period of 152nd Chakra is obtained. 24068.25+2022.97=26091.22 years are obtained i.e. 152nd Chakra will end at midnight of 20th March in the year 26092 AD.

Chakra Bhukta Year Calculation Vikrami Samvat:- 1702.69 Bhukta Varshadi, 1702.69 Nirayan years ago, 152nd Chakra started or by subtracting Bhukta years from Ishtavarsha, the starting period of 152nd Chakra is obtained, 2079.69-1702.69=377 years. 1st entry Baisakha 152nd Chakra started on Samvat 378 Vikrami.

Chakra Bhogya Varsha Calculation:- 24068.31 By adding Bhogya Varshadi to Ishtavarsha, the completion period of 152nd Chakra is obtained. 24068.31+2079.69=26148 years were obtained i.e. the 152nd Chakra will end on the midnight of 30th Pravisht Chaitra on Samvat 26149 Vikrami.

Chakra Bhukta Year Calculation Shaka Samvat:- 1702.75 Bhukta Varshadi, 1702.75 Sayan years ago, 152nd Chakra started or by subtracting Bhukta years from Ishtavarsha, the starting period of 152nd Chakra is obtained, Ishtavarsha 1944.75-1702.75=242 years. 1st entry Chaitra, The 152nd cycle started on Samvat 243 Shaka.

Chakra Bhogya Varsha Calculation:- 24068.25 By adding Bhogya Varshadi to Ishtavarsha, the completion period of 152nd Chakra is obtained. 24068.25+1944.75=26013 years obtained i.e. the 152nd Chakra will end on the midnight of 30th entry Phalgun on Samvat 26014 Shaka.

Hari Om

CHAPTER FIFTEEN

NIRAYAN SANKRANTIES FROM SEASONS CHANGE

To calculate in which month, day and season the Meshadi Sankranti of the Nirayan Sun took place on the day of the end of Triyuga, convert the seasonal change days into month decimals, similarly make the months decimal of the months like 21st March etc., add both. On Nirayan Meshadi Sankranti month decimals are obtained. If it is more than 12 then subtract 12, the remainder is less than 0,1 respectively and the months are January, February etc. and by multiplying the digits after the decimal with the average of the month, the last date of the month (January etc.) is obtained.

Before finding the Nirayan Sankranti date, read and understand this article thoroughly. First of all find out the Ayanamsha, divide the Ayanamsha by 30 and get the Sayana Rashi. This Sayan zodiac sign is passing in front of the first point of the Nirayan Aries zodiac sign located at Bhachakra in a clockwise direction or the starting point of the first entry of the month of Baishakh.

Example:- Ayanamsha of 151st Chakra was 312.21 decimal fraction, dividing by 30 gave 10.41 Rashi or Sayan Aquarius. Sayan Aquarius is passing before the first point of Nirayan Aries or Baishakh month.

Sayan Sign, Month, Season, Sankranti Date and Month Decimal Table.					
S.Sign	Seasonal Date	Season	Sk.date	Sk.MD	Sayan Mass
Pisces	19Feb to 20March	Spring	19 Feb	1.64	Phalgun
Aries	21March to 19April	Spring	21 Mar	2.65	Chaitra
Taurus	20April to 20May	Summer	20 April	3.63	Baisakh
Gemini	21May to 20June	Summer	21 May	4.65	Jyestha
Cancer	21June to 22July	Rain	21 June	5.67	Ashadh
Leo	23July to 22Aug	Rain	23 July	6.71	Shravan
Virgo	23Aug to 22Sep	Autumn	23 Aug	7.71	Bhadrapada
Libra	23Sep to 23Oct	Autumn	23 Sep	8.73	Ashwin
Scorpio	23Oct to 21Nov	Pre-winter	23 Oct	9.71	Kartik
Sagittarius	22Nov to 21Dec	Pre-winter	22 Nov	10.70	Margsheesh
Capricorn	22Dec to 19Jan	Winter	22 Dec	11.68	Paush
Aquarius	20Jan to 18Feb	Winter	20 Jan	0.61	Magha

Nirayan Sign, Month table.	
Narayan Rashi	Month
Aries	Baisakh
Taurus	Jyestha
Gemini	Ashadh
Cancer	Sravan
Leo	Bhadrapada
Virgo	Ashwin
Libra	Kartik
Scorpio	Margshirsh
Sagittarius	Paush
Capricorn	Magha
Aquarius	Phalgun
Pisces	Chaitra

- See the table of Sayan Rashi, Month, Season, etc., the first column is of Sayan Rashi. Now we had found out the Sayan Aquarius zodiac sign, in the table the dominance of the Aquarius zodiac sign is from 20th January to 18th February and in the middle of this is the winter season, this is the zodiac sign starting from the Sayan Sankranti date 20th January or 0.61 month Decimal or Sayan Magha month.

- If we include the entry 12.39 obtained from the second column of the Bhukta-Bhogya table given below in 20th January or count 13 days (12.39) from 20th January, then the date of 2nd February will be obtained. Its the meaning is that during the end of Dwaparyug, Nirayan Varsharambh or Baishakh Sankranti used to occur on 2nd February. In the table, Shishir (Winter) Ritu, Sayan Magh month etc. are being obtained from 2nd February, 20th January to 18th February. Like currently according to Vikrami Samvat, the years is starting from 14th April. In the table, falling between 14th April, 21st March and 19th April is giving the month of Sayan Aries, Spring season and Sayan Chaitra month.

- Nirayan Baishakh Sankranti is starting from 2nd February or it can also be said that before the first entry of Baishakh, 12.39 or 13th Pravistha of Sayan Magh month is active. Winter season is left till the end of Sayan Magh. As soon as Sayan Phalguna begins, spring will arrive. There are

30.44-12.39=18.05 days left for Falgun to occur.

- To find out the Sankranti of Nirayan Rashi equivalent to Sayan Rashi, add the month decimal given in the fifth column from Sayan Rashi in the table Sayan Rashi, Month, Season, etc., to Sayan Rashi. If this sum is more than 12, then subtract 12. This result is obtained in the form of the month of January etc. In the total result, multiply the digits after the decimal with the total days of the respective month to calculate the days-hours etc.

- **Example:-** In the table, Sayan Sankranti of Aquarius sign is 20th January and its month decimal. Received 0.61. By adding 10.41 to month decimal 0.61, 11.02 month (December) was obtained. Rounding off 0.02 digits after the decimal gives 1 December, 14 hours, 50 minutes and 33.83 seconds. In the table, falling between 1st December, 22nd November to 21st December, Sayan Sagittarius, Hemant (Pre-Winter) Ritu and Sayan Margashirsha month is being received.

- **Note,** 0.61 Sayan Kumbh Sankranti month is decimal, by adding the decimal of 10.41 months of the seasons till the said period, the Nirayan Aquarius equivalent to Sayan Rashi is reached. The interval between Sayan and Nirayan zodiac signs is 48.49 days. Above Nirayan Rashi, Month Table, Phalgun month is obtained from Nirayan Aquarius.

Ganavarshaadi Bhukta-Bhogya table.		
	(a) Ganavarsha	(b) Ganavarsha
Bhukta/Bhogya	316.77 Bhokta	48.49 Bhogya
R P Varsadi	0.87 or 0.09	0.13
Mass	10.41	1.59
Pravistha	12.39	18.05

Example, Part-1:- Triyuga End Season Change Day 316.77/(365.256363/12)=10.41 Month.

Aquarius Sankranti (Phalgun): - See the above Sayan table, in the Sayan Aquarius sign and month decimal column, the month decimal of 20th January is given as 0.61, if it is added to 10.41 Bhukta month decimal, then 11.02 (December) is obtained, the decimal will be given in the next digit. Month multiplied by average value 0.02×31=0.62 days, decimal 0.62×24=14.84 hours, decimal 0.84×60=50.56 minutes, decimal 0.56×60=33.83 seconds decimal, i.e. in the end of Triyuga. Nirayan

Kumbha Sankranti was taking place on December 1 at 14:50 minutes and 33.83 seconds decimal.

Kumbh Sankranti is currently at a distance of 48.49 days (Bhogya month 1.59) from its target (equivalence) point, this means that there is a distance of 48.49 days between Nirayan Kumbh Sankranti and Sayan Kumbh Sankranti, 48.49 days in annual motion and 48.49 days in Sayan motion. Consider the distance equivalent to years obtained by multiplying the above days by 70.56 days. For this reason the seasons also move away from the same ratio. In the above Sayan table season determination column, 1st December is between 22nd November to 21st December, hence Hemant (Pre-winter) Ritu, Sayan Sagittarius and Sayan Margashirsha are obtained. In the Nirayan zodiac and month table, the month of Phalgun is being received from Aquarius. Take a decision by looking at the tables further. The distance of 48.49 is clear between 1st December and 20th January.

Pisces Sankranti (Chaitra):- 19 February month decimal 1.64+10.41=12.05-12=0.05 (January), 0.05×31=1.55 days, decimal 0.55×24=13.13 hours, decimal 0.13×60=7.71 minutes, the digits after decimal are 0.71×60=42.40 seconds decimal, that is, during the end of Triyug, Nirayan Pisces Sankranti was happening on 2nd January at 13:00, 7 minutes and 42.40 seconds decimal, on 2nd January was the winter and Chaitra Nirayan month.

Aries Sankranti (Baishakh):- 21 March Mass Decimal 2.65+10.41-13.05-12-1.05 (February), 0.05×28=1.46 day, decimal 0.46×24=11.08 hours, decimal 0.08×60-5.03 minutes, decimal 0.03×60-1.52 seconds decimal, that is, during the end of Triyuga, Nirayan Aries Sankanti will be on 2 February at 11 AM, 5 Minutes and 1.52 seconds were in decimal, February 2 was the month of Shishir Ritu and Baishakh Nirayan.

Taurus Sankranti (Jyeshtha):- 20th April month decimal 3.63+10.41=14.04-12=2.04 (March), 0.05×31=1.25 days, decimal 0.25×24=6.04 hours, decimal 0.04×60=2.56 minutes, the figures after decimal are 0.56×60=33.83 seconds decimal, that is, during the end of Triyuga, Nirayan Vrish Sankranti was happening on March 2 at 6:02 minutes and 33.83 seconds decimal, March 2 was the spring season and

Jyeshtha solar month.

Gemini Sankranti (Ashadha):- 21 May month decimal 4.65+10.41=15.06-12=3.05 (April), 0.05×30=1.57 days, decimal 0.57×24=13.59 hours, decimal 0.59×60=35.38 minutes , the numbers after decimal are 0.38×60=23.06 seconds decimal, that is, during the end of Triyug, Nirayan Mithun Sankranti was happening on April 2 at 13:35 minutes and 23.06 seconds decimal, April 2 was spring season and Ashadha solar month.

Cancer Sankranti (Shravan):- Season change 316.77/(365.256363/ 12)=10.41 month, 20/30+5=5.67, 21 June Month decimal, 10.41+5.67=16.08-12=4.07 (May), decimal 0.07×30=2.29 days, decimal 0.29×24=6.84 hours, decimal 0.84×60=50.56 minutes, decimal

0.56×60=33.83 seconds decimal, i.e. Nirayana Karka Sankranti on May 3 at the end of the Triyuga It was 6 o'clock, 50 minutes and 33.83 seconds in decimal, May 3 was summer season and Shravan solar month.

Leo Sankranti (Bhadrapada):- 316.77/(365.256363/12)=10.41, 22/ 31+6=6.71, 23 July month decimal, 10.41+6.71=17.12-12=5.12 (June), 0.12×30=3.50 days, Post-decimal digits 0.50×24=12.04 hours, post-decimal digits 0.04×60=2.48 minutes, post-decimal digits 0.48×60=28.87 seconds decimal, i.e. It was happening in 12:02minutes and 28.87 seconds decimal, June 4 was summer season and Bhadrapada solar month.

Virgo Sankranti (Ashwin):- 316.77/(365.256363/12)=10.41, 22/ 31+7=7.71, 23 August month decimal, 10.41+7.71=18.12-12=6.12 (July), 0.12×31=3.62 days, decimal later Numbers 0.62×24=14.84 hours, numbers after decimal 0.84×60=50.56 minutes, numbers after decimal 0.56×60=33.83 seconds decimal, i.e. Nirayan Kanya Sankranti during the end of Triyuga on 4th July at 14:00, 50 minutes and 33.83 seconds decimal. It was happening on 4th July, it was the rainy season and Ashwin solar month.

Libra Sankranti (Kartik):- 316.77/(365.256363/12)=10.41, 22/ 30+8=8.73, 23 September. Decimal, 10.11+8.73=19.12-12=7.14 (August), 0.14×31=4.35 days, 0.35×24=8.44 hours, 0.44×60=26.56 minutes, 0.56×60=33.83 seconds decimal, i.e. during the end of Triyuga, Nirayan

Tula Sankranti was happening on 5th August at 8:26 AM and 33.83 seconds decimal, 5th August was the rainy season and Kartik solar month.

Scorpio Sankranti (Margashirsha):- 316.77/(365.256363/12)=10.41, 22/30+9=9.71, 23 October month decimal, 10.41+9.71=20.12-12=8.12 (September), 0.12×30=3.5 days, post-decimal digits 0.5×24=12.04 hours, post-decimal digits 0.4×60=2.48 minutes, post-decimal digits 0.48×60=28.87 seconds decimal, that is, the Nirayana Scorpio conjunction at the end of the Triyuga was occurring at 12 o'clock, 2 minutes and 28.87 seconds decimal on September 4. 4th September was the autumn and Margarshish solar month.

Sagittarius Sankranti (Paush):- 316.77/(365.256363/12)=10.41, 21/30+10=10.70, 22 November month decimal, 10.41+10.7=21.11-12=9.11 (October), 0.11×31=3.32 days, Decimal figures 0.32×24=7.64 hours, Decimal figures 0.64×60=38.56 minutes, Decimal figures 0.56×60=33.83 seconds Decimal, i.e. Nirayan Dhanu Sankranti during the end of Triyug will be on October 4 at 7:00, 38 minutes and It was 33.83 seconds in decimal, October 4 was Sharad (Autumn) and Paush solar month.

Capricorn Sankranti (Magh):- 316.77/(365.256363/12)=10.41, 21/30+11=11.68, December month decimal, 10.41+11.68=22.08-12=10.08 (November), digits after decimal 0.08×30=2.53 Day, digits after decimal 0.53×24=12.82 hours, digits after decimal 0.82×60=48.93 minutes, digits after decimal 0.93×60=55.96 seconds decimal, i.e. Nirayan Makar Sankranti during the end of Triyuga on 3rd November at 12 o'clock, 48 Minutes and 55.96 seconds were in decimal, 3rd November was Hemanta (Pre-winter) season and Magha solar month.

Note, the example of Part-2 or 3421 (B) Ganavarsha, Ayanamsha Shunyakaal is not being given, because it will have to be calculated by adding 22350 (A) Ganavarsha and 3421 (B) Ganavarsha, which will be the sum of 25771 years of the cycle, That is, Ayanamsh will be zero and in the Ayanamsh zero period, Syan Sankanti will be received on 21st March, 20th April etc.

End of Dwapara Yuga Sankranti Table.						
Sayan Sign	Aquarius	Pisces	Aries	Taurus	Gemini	Cancer
Season	Winter	Spring	Spring	Summer	Summer	Rain
Sayan Month	Magh	Falgun	Chaitra	Baisakh	Jyestha	Ashadha
Bhukta Pravistha	12.39	12.39	12.39	12.39	12.39	12.39
Bhogya Pravistha	18.05	18.05	18.05	18.05	18.05	18.05
Nirayan Sign	Aries	Taurus	Gemini	Cancer	Leo	Virgo
Sankranti Mass	Baisakh	Jyestha	Ashadha	Sravan	Bhadrapad	Ashwin
Month	Feb	March	April	May	June	July
Nir. Sankranti Date	1.46	1.25	1.57	2.29	3.50	3-62
Date	2	2	2	3	4	4

Sayan Sign	Leo	Virgo	Libra	Scorpio	Sagittarius	Capricorn
Season	Rain	Autumn	Autumn	P.Winter	P.Winter	Winter
Sayan Month	Sravan	Bhadrapad	Ashwin	Kartika	Margshirsh	Pausha
Bhukta Pravistha	12.39	12.39	12.39	12.39	12.39	12.39
Bhogya Pravistha	18.05	18.05	18.05	18.05	18.05	18.05
Nirayan Sign	Libra	Scorpio	Sagittarius	Capricorn	Aquarius	Pisces
Sankranti Mass	Kartika	Margshirsh	Pausha	Magh	Falgun	Chaitra
Month	August	September	October	November	December	January
Nir. Sankranti Date	4.35	3.50	3.32	2.53	0.62	1.55
Date	5	4	4	3	1	2

Season Change Bhukta-Bhogya table.		
	(a) Ganavarsha	(b) Ganavarsha
Bhukta/Bhogya	316.77 Bhokta	48.49 Bhogya
R P Varsadi	0.87 or 0.09	0.13
Month	10.41	1.59
Pravistha	12.39	18.05
Hours	9.35	1.16
Minutes	21.17	9.60

See the above table, at the end of Dwaparayuga, Ayanamsha was of Aquarius, hence the first row has been started from Sayan Rashi Aquarius, this also means that Sayan was in front of Aquarius, Nirayan Aries or Baishakh solar month. Sayan Aquarius falls under the autumn season from January 20 to February 19. If we count the Bhukta entries from 20th January till 12.39, then clearly 1.46 or 2nd February is falling in front of Nirayan Aries. If we add 18.05 to the above date of February 1.46 then we get the date 19.51 or 20 or this is the starting date of Sayan Pisces, understand further in this way.

Example, Part-3:- 22 January 2023, season change day, 24.13/(365.256363/12)=0.79 months.

Aries Sankranti (Baishakh):- Seasonal change month 0.79+2.65=3.44 (April) month decimal, 0.44×30=13.14 days, decimal 0.14×24=3.38 hours, decimal 0.38×60=22.92 minutes, The digits after decimal are 0.92×60=55.04 seconds decimal, that is, currently Nirayan Aries Sankranti is happening on 13.14 or 14 April at 3:22 minutes and 55.04 seconds decimal. April 14 is the spring season, falling before the solar month of Nirayan Aries and Baishakh, between March 21 and April 20.

Taurus Sankanti (Jyeshtha):- Season change month 0.79+3.63=4.43 (May) month decimal, 0.43×31=13.21 days, decimal 0.21×24=5.09 hours, decimal 0.09×60=5.68 minutes, The digits after decimal are 0.68×60=40.88 seconds decimal, that is, currently Nirayan Vrish Sankranti is happening on 13.21 or 14 May at 5:05 minutes and 40.88 seconds decimal. Summer season is falling between 20th April to 21st May, in front of Nirayan Taurus and Jyeshtha solar month.

Gemini Sankranti (Ashadha):- Season change month 0.79+4.65=5.44 (June) month decimal, 0.44×30=13.14 days, decimal 0.14×24=3.38 hours, decimal 0.38×60=22.92 minutes, The numbers after decimal are 0.92×60=55.04 seconds decimal, i.e. currently Nirayan Mithun Sankranti is occurring on 14th June in 3:22 minutes and 55.04 seconds decimal. June 14, summer season is falling in front of Nirayan Gemini and Ashadha solar month between May 21 and June 21.

Cancer Sankranti (Shravan):- Season change month 0.79+5.67=6.46 (July) Month decimal, 0.46×31=14.25 days, digits after decimal 0.25×24=5.89 hours, digits after decimal 0.89×60= 53.68 minutes, digits after decimal The numbers are 0.68×60=40.88 seconds decimal, that is, currently Nirayan Cancer Sankanti is happening on 15th July at 5:53 minutes and 40.88 seconds decimal. The rainy season is falling on 15th July between 21st June to 23rd July, in front of Nirayan Cancer and Shravan solar month.

Leo Sankranti (Bhadrapada):- Season change month 0.79+6.71=7.50 (August) month decimal, 0.50×31=15.58 days, decimal 0.58×24=13.89 hours, decimal 0.89×60=53.68 minutes, The digits after the decimal are 0.68×60=40.88 seconds decimal, that is, currently Nirayan Singh Sankranti is happening on 16th August at 13:53 minutes and 40.88 seconds decimal. Nirayan Singh and Bhadrapada solar month 16th August is falling between 23rd July to 23rd August, rainy season.

Virgo Sankanti (Ashwin):- Seasonal Change Month 0.79+7.71=8.50 (September) Month Decimal, Decimal Later 0.50×30=15.08 days, decimal 0.08×24=1.83 hours, decimal 0.83×60= 50.01 minutes, decimal

0.01×60=0.85 seconds, that is, currently Nirayan Kanya Sankranti 16 It is happening on September at 1:50 minutes and 0.85 seconds in decimal. Autumn season is falling on 16th September in front of Nirayan Kanya and Ashwin solar month between 23rd August to 23rd September.

Libra Sankranti (Kartik):- Season change month 0.79+8.73=9.53 (October) month decimal, after decimal 0.53×31=16.31 days, decimal 0.31×24=7.49 hours, decimal 0.49×60=29.68 minutes, decimal 0.68×60=40.88 seconds decimal, that is, currently Nirayan Tula Sankranti 17 It is happening on October at 7:29 minutes and 40.88 seconds in decimal. Autumn season is falling on 17th October between 23rd September to 23rd October, in front of Nirayana Tula and Kartik solar month.

Scorpio Sankranti (Margashirsha):- Seasonal Change Month 0.79+9.71=10.50 (November) Month Decimal, Decimal 0.50×30=15.08 days, 0.08×24=1.83 hours, 0.83×60=50.01 minutes, 0.01×60=0.85 seconds decimal, i.e. currently Nirayan Scorpio Sankranti It is happening on 16th November at 1:50 minutes and 0.85 seconds in decimal. 16th November, Hemant (Pre-Winter) ritu, is falling in front of Nirayana Scorpio and Margashirsha solar month between 23rd October to 22nd November.

Sagittarius Sankranti (Paush):- Season change month 0.79+10.70=11.49 (December) month decimal, 0.49×31=15.28 days, decimal 0.28×24=6.69 hours, decimal 0.69×60=41.68 minutes, The numbers after decimal are 0.68×60=40.88 seconds decimal, that is, currently Nirayan Dhanu Sankranti is happening on 16th December at 6:41 minutes and 40.88 seconds decimal. Hemant (Pre-Winter) ritu, is falling on 16th December between 22nd November to 22nd December in front of Nirayan Sagittarius and Paush solar month.

Capricorn Sankranti (Magh):- Season Change Mass 0.79+11.68=12.47-12=0.47 (January) Mass Decimal, Figures after decimal 0.47×31=14.58 days, Figures after decimal 0.58×24=13.89 hours, Figures after decimal 0.89×60=53.68 minutes, Figures after decimal 0.68×60=40.88 seconds decimal, i.e. currently Nirayan Makar Sankranti is happening on January 15 at 13:53 minutes and 40.88 seconds decimal. Shishir (Winter) Ritu is falling on 15th January in front of Nirayan Makar and Magh solar months between 22nd December to 20th January.

Aquarius Sankranti (Phalgun):- Season change month 0.79+0.61=1.41 (February) month decimal, 0.41×28=11.36 days, decimal 0.36×24=8.68 hours, decimal 0.68×60=40.74 minutes, The numbers after decimal are 0.74×60=44.66 seconds decimal, that is, currently Nirayan Kumbh Sankranti is happening on 12th February at 8:40 minutes and 44.66 seconds decimal. Shishir (Winter) Ritu is falling on 12 February, in front of Nirayan Kumbh and Phalgun solar month between 20 January to 19 February.

Pisces Sankranti (Chaitra):- Season change month 0.79+1.64=2.44 (March) month decimal, 0.44×31=13.51 days, decimal 0.51×24=12.18 hours, decimal 0.18×60=10.82 minutes, The figures after decimal are 0.82×60=49.45 seconds decimal, that is, currently Nirayan Pisces Sankranti is happening on March 14 at 12:10 AM and 49.45 seconds decimal. March 14 is the spring season falling in front of Nirayan Pisces and Chaitra solar month between 19th February to 21st March.

Current Sankranti Table.						
Sayan Sign	Aries	Taurus	Gemini	Cancer	Leo	Virgo
Season	Spring	Summer	Summer	Rain	Rain	Autumn
Sayan Month	Chaitra	Baisakh	Jyestha	Ashadha	Sravan	Bhadrapad
Bhukta Pravistha	24.13	24.13	24.13	24.13	24.13	24.13
Bhogya Pravistha	6.30	6.30	6.30	6.30	6.30	6.30
Nirayan Sign	Aries	Taurus	Gemini	Cancer	Leo	Virgo
Sankranti Mass	Baisakh	Jyestha	Ashadha	Sravan	Bhadrapad	Ashwin
Month	April	May	June	July	August	September
Nir. Sankranti Date	13.14	13.21	13.14	14.25	15.58	15.08
Date	14	14	14	15	16	16

Sayan Sign	Libra	Scorpio	Sagittarius	Capricorn	Aquarius	Pisces
Season	Autumn	P.Winter	P.Winter	Winter	Winter	Spring
Sayan Month	Ashwin	Kartika	Margshirsh	Pausha	Magh	Falgun
Bhukta Pravistha	24.13	24.13	24.13	24.13	24.13	24.13
Bhogya Pravistha	6.30	6.30	6.30	6.30	6.30	6.30
Nirayan Sign	Libra	Scorpio	Sagittarius	Capricorn	Aquarius	Pisces
Sankranti Mass	Kartika	Margshirsh	Pausha	Magh	Falgun	Chaitra
Month	October	November	December	January	February	March
Nir. Sankranti Date	16.31	15.08	15.28	14.58	11.36	13.51
Date	17	16	16	15	12	14

Season Change Bhukta-Bhogya table.		
	(c) Ganavarsha	(c) Ganavarsha
Bhukta/Bhogya	24.13 Bhokta	341.13 Bhogya
R P Varsadi	0.7	0.93
Month	0.79	11.21
Pravistha	24.13	6.30
Hours	3.15	7.37
Minutes	9.15	21.16

See the above table, currently Ayanamsha is of Aries, hence the first row has been started from Sayan Rashi Aries, this also means that Sayan Aries is in front of Nirayan Aries or Baishakh solar month. Sayan Aries zodiac dates i.e. from March 21 to April 20 fall under the spring season. If we count the Bhukta entries from 21st March till 24.13, then clearly 13.14 or 14th April will fall in front of Nirayan Aries. If the above April 13.14 date is added with 6.30 Bhogya entry, then 19.44 or 20 date is obtained, this is the starting date of Sayan Taurus, that is, after 6.3 or 7 days or from the 7th entry of Vaishakh month, Sayan Taurus summer season will arrive. This is said for annual speed, for Sayan speed, 6.3 has to be multiplied by 70.56 years and included in Ishtavarsha, understand further in this way.

6.3×70.56=444.83+2022.97 Ishtavarsha=2467.8 years, currently Ayanamsha is of Aries, but from the year 2468 AD, Baishakh solar month will start in Sayan Taurus and summer season (April 20). Therefore, keep in mind, in annual motion, 6.3 days after April 14 and in Sayan Chakra motion, Sayan Taurus and summer season will begin after 444.83 years from the present. Under the annual movement, Sankranti remains on the same date for 70.56 years, this adds up to a micro period.

Other examples:- Another example of 21 March 1956, Seasonal Change 23.17 regarding main Sankanti.

Seasonal change table.	
Ganavarsha	Ganavarsha
23.17 Bhukta	342.08 Bhogya
0.6	0.94
0.76	11.24
23.17	7.26

Aries Sankranti (Baishakh):- Seasonal change month 0.76+2.65=3.41 (April) month decimal, 0.41×30=12.19 days, i.e. currently Nirayan Aries Sankranti was on 12.19 or 13 April. April 13 is the spring season, falling before the solar month of Nirayan Aries and Baishakh, between March 21 and April 20.

Cancer Sankranti (Shravan):- Seasonal change month 0.76+5.67=6.43 (July) Month decimal, 0.43×31=13.27 days, i.e. currently Nirayan Kark Sankranti was happening on 14th July. 14th July is the rainy season falling in front of Nirayan Cancer and Shravan solar month between 21st June to 23rd July.

Libra Sankranti (Kartik):- Seasonal change month 0.76+8.73=9.49 (October) month decimal, digits after decimal 0.49×31=15.33 days, that is, currently Nirayan Tula Sankranti was happening on 16 October. Autumn season is falling on 16th October between 23rd September to 23rd October, in front of Nirayana Tula and Kartik solar month.

Capricorn Sankranti (Magh):- Season change month 0.76+11.68=12.44-12=0.44 (January) Month decimal, digits after decimal 0.44×31=13.60 days, i.e. currently Nirayan Makar Sankranti was happening on 14 January. Shishir (Winter) Ritu is falling on 14th January in front of Nirayan Makar and Magh solar months between 22nd December to 20th January.

Main Sankranti				
Sayan Sign	Aries	Cancer	Libra	Capricorn
Season	Spring	Rain	Autumn	Winter
Sayan Month	Chaitra	Ashadha	Ashwin	Paush
Bhukta Pravistha	23.17	23.17	23.17	23.17
Bhogya Pravistha	7.26	7.26	7.26	7.26
Nirayan Sign	Aries	Cancer	Libra	Capricorn
Sankranti Mass	Baisakh	Sravan	Kartik	Magh
Month	April	July	October	January
Nir. Sankranti Date	12.19	13.27	15.3	13.60
Date	13	14	16	14

Ayanamsha and Nirayan Sankranti					
Ayan.	21Mar-East	21June-North	23Sep-West	22Dec-South	AD
0°	Aries	Cancer	Libra	Capricorn	320.22
90°	Capricorn	Aries	Cancer	Libra	6762.56
180°	Libra	Capricorn	Aries	Cancer	13205.11
270°	Cancer	Libra	Capricorn	Aries	19647.67
360°	Aries	Cancer	Libra	Capricorn	26090.22

See the above Ayanamsh and Nirayan Sankranti table, 21st March moves towards East, 21st June towards North, 23rd September towards West and 22nd December towards South. On zero/360 degrees ayanamsha, Aries is towards the east, Cancer towards the north, Libra towards the west and Capricorn towards the south. Thereafter, as the Ayanamsha increases, the Sayan and Meshaadi zodiac signs rotate in the clockwise direction. Due to which in the year 6763 AD, when 90 degrees Ayanamsha occurs, Makar Sankranti will start happening on 21 March, Baisakhi on 21 June, Cancer Sankranti on 23 September and Tula Sankranti on 22 December. Understand in the same way in future also.

Just as the annual seasonal cycle moves for humans on land, in the same way for the gods, their annual seasonal cycle is 25771 years for us, 6442.75 years are 3 month.

In some previous chapter, it was written about the Sun's radiance, for the sake of context, I am saying it in detail here also, first of all, remember that the long form of the annual motion is Sayan Chakra motion, it is possible that the Sun is even smaller than the annual motion. Let the daily speed be. The Sun rises in the east and sets in the west, the same happens in both the above mentioned movements, the only difference is that in the daily motion we clearly see the Sun rising in the east and setting in the west (180 degrees approximately), the rest 180 degrees are not visible, meaning the 360 degree circle is complete.

Whereas in annual and sayan motion, it is similar to daily motion, but in annual motion it appears to move only 90 degrees north or south from the east, whereas in sayan motion it is not possible to see. The purpose of all these things is that all motion is complete through 360 degrees. Daily speed is very small, annual speed is small and sayan speed is long time calculation units.

Sayan Sankranti and Season are based on their fixed dates, hence I do not feel the need to give the example of Sayan Sankranti. On the basis of Bhukta-Bhogya entries given above, the distance between Nirayana and Sayan has been made clear. 21st March etc. Sayan dates and seasons are dynamic, as many days will be the change of seasons, there will be the same distance between Nirayan Sankanti and 21st March etc. dates.

Hari Om

CHAPTER SIXTEEN

REVERSE CALCULATION OF AYANAMSHA OF AYANAMSAKARTAS

The purpose here is that even by reverse calculation of Ayanamsh, Ritu Parivartan Dinadi, Nirayan Meshadi Sankanti, current Kalisamvat can be brought. On March 12, 2024, at 23:00, 7 minutes, 15.01 seconds, 5124 years of Kali Samvat will be completed, after which the 5125th Samvat will begin. In the above calculations, the years of Kalisamvat have also been proved and shown.

Here, from 17th November 2023, Ayanamsha 23.78 degrees, we find out the difference by doing reverse calculations taking different Ayanamshas. For convenience, the month of March 21 has been given as 2.65 and 0.22 decimal years, Kalisamvat as 5123.59 years and Ayanamsha zero year as 320.22.

By differentiating the Ayanamsha and other Ayanamshas of this book and multiplying by 71.59 years, the difference Varshadi is obtained. This difference will be the difference of Ayanamsh zero years between the two. If the Ayanamsh is less than the other Ayanamshas, then difference years will have to be subtracted from 320.22 Varshadi, but if the Ayanamsh of the book is more then difference years will have to be added to 320.22.

Formulas:-

- **Difference years:-** Ayanamsha Difference (×)71.59years.
- **Ayanasha zero year:-** 320.22 (-) or (+) Difference years.
- **Ganavarsha:-** Ayanasha fraction decimal(×)25771/360.
- **Seasonal Change Days:-** Ganavarsha×365.256363/25771.
- **Refinement Year:-** Seasonal Change Month Decimal (+) 21 March Month Decimal (/) 12.
- **Kali Samvat:-** 3421.22 (+) Ganavarsha (-) Shodhana.
- **Aries Sankranti:-** Seasonal Change Month Decimal (+) 21March Month Decimal = Aries Sankranti Month Decimal, Decimal Later Digits etc. Related Month Total Days = Aries Sankranti Date.

Example 1:Lahari Ayanamsha:- 24°11′24″ or 24.19° decimal, November 17, 2023AD.

Difference years:- Debt difference of 24.19-23.78=0.41×71.59=29.01 (-) difference years, consider it as 29 years.

Ayanamsha zero years:- Ayanasha is a debt, so it must be subtracted, 320.22-29=291.22 Ayanasha zero year.

Ganavarsha:- 24.19×25771/360=1731.67 Ganavarsha.

Seasonal Change Days:- 1731.67×365.256363/25771=24.54 Days Seasonal Change.

Refinement year:- 24:54/(365.256363/12)/12+0.22 (21March) = 0.29 year decimal.

Kali Samvat:- 3421.22+1731.67-0.29 years=5152.60 Kali Samvat.

Aries Sankranti:- Seasonal Decimal 24.54/(365.256363/12)=0.81+2.65=3.45 April, 0.45×30= 13.54 days, i.e. Nirayan Aries Sankranti occurs on 14th April, Baishakh month, spring season.

Season change Decimal digits 0.54×70.56=38.33 years, only on 14th April for last 38.33 years

Nirayan Aries Sankranti is occurring and will continue to occur for 70.56-38.33=32.23 years.

The spent years were subtracted from the Ishtavarsha 2022.88 (17 November 2023 AD), 2022.88-38.33=1984.55 years, on 20 July 1985 AD, Nirayan Aries Sankranti started from 7 o'clock, 29.11 minutes on 14 April. Bhogya years were added to Ishtavarsha 2022.88, 2022.88+32.23=2055.11 year, on 9 February 2056 AD, Nirayan Taurus Sankranti will start from 5:35.92 AM on 15 April.

Example 2: Raman Ayanamsha:- 22°44'46" or 22.75° decimal, 17 November 2023AD.

Difference years:- 23.78-22.75=1.04×71.59=74.35 years (+) difference.

Ayanamsha zero year:- Ayanamsha is (+), hence it has to be added, 320.22+74.35=394.57 Ayanamsha Zero Years.

Ganavarsha:- 22.75×25771/360=1628.58 Ganavarsha.

Seasonal change days:- 1628.58×365.256363/25771=23.08 days seasonal change.

Refinement year:- 23.08/(365.256363/12)/12+0.22 (21March) = 0.28 year decimal.

Kalisamvat:- 3421.22+1628.58-0.28 refinement=5049.52 Kalisamvat.

Aries Sankranti:- Seasonal Change Decimals 23.08/(365.256363/12)=0.76+2.65=3.40 April, 0.4×30=12.10 days, i.e. Nirayan Aries Sankranti occurs on 13th April, Baishakh month, spring season. Seasonal Changes Decimal Numbers 0.08×70.56=5.8 years, Nirayan Aries Sankranti is happening on 13th April for the last 5.80 years and will continue to happen for 70.56-5.80=64.76 years.

Example 3: KP (Old) Ayanamsha:- 24°05'44" or 24.10° decimal, November 17, 2023 AD.

Difference years:- 24.10-23.78=0.31×71.59=22.25 years (-) difference.

Ayanamsha zero year:- Ayanamsh is a minus, hence it has to be subtracted, 320.22-22.25= 297.97 Ayanamsh zero years.

Ganavarsha:- 24.1×25771/360=1725.23 Ganavarsha.

Seasonal change days:- 1725.23×365.256363/25771=24.45 days seasonal change.

Refinement year:- 24.45/(365.256363/12)/12+0.22 (21 March)=0.29 year decimal.

Kalisamvat:- 3421.22+1725.23-0.29 refinement=5146.16 Kalisamvat.

Aries Sankranti:- Seasonal Change Decimal 24.45/(365.256363/12)=0.80+2.65=3.45 April,

0.45×30=13.45 days, i.e. Nirayan Aries Sankranti occurs on 14th April, Baishakh month, spring season. Seasonal change decimal digits 0.45×70.56=31.88 years, Nirayan Aries Sankranti is happening on 14th April for the last 31.88 years and will continue to happen for 70.56-31.88=38.67 years.

Example 4: KP (New) Ayanmsh:- 24°05′59″ or 24.10° decimal, 17 November 2023 AD.

Difference years:- 24.10-23.78=0.31×71.59=22.55 years (-) decimal.

Ayanamsh Zero Time:- Ayanamsh is a minus, hence it has to be subtracted, 320.22-22.55= 297.67 Ayanamsh Zero Time.

Ganavarsha:- 24.1×25771/360=1725.23 Ganavarsha.

Seasonal Change Days:- 1725.23×365.256363/25771=24.45 Days Seasonal Change.

Refinement year:- 24.45/(365.256363/12)/12+0.22 (21 March) = 0.29 years decimal.

Kalisamvat:- 3421.22+1725.23-0.29 Ref.years = 5146.16 Kalisamvat.

Aries Sankranti:- Seasonal Change Decimal 24.45/(365.256363/12)=0.80+2.65=3.45 April,

0.45×30=13.45 days, i.e. Nirayan Aries Sankranti occurs on 14th April, Baishakh month, spring season. Season change Decimal digits 0.45×70.56=31.88 years, last 31.88 years on 14th April only, Nirayan Aries Sankranti is occurring and will continue to occur for 70.56-31.88=38.67 years.

Example 5: Khullar Ayanamsh:- 24°10'46" or 24.18° decimal, 17 November 2023 AD.

Difference years:- 24.18-23.78=0.39×71.59=28.26 years (-) difference.

Ayanamsh Zero Time:- Ayanamsh is a minus, hence it has to be subtracted, 320.22-28.26= 291.97 Ayanamsh Zero Time.

Ganavarsha:- 24.18×25771/360=1730.95 Ganavarsha.

Seasonal Change Days:- 1730.95×365.256363/25771=24.53 days seasonal change.

Refinement year:- 24.53/(365.256363/12)/12+0.22 (21 March) = 0.29 year decimal.

Kalisamvat:- 3421.22+1730.95-0.29 refinement=5151.89 Kalisamvat.

Aries Sankanti:- Seasonal change decimal 24.53/(365.256363/12)=0.81+2.65=3.45 April, 0.45×30=13.53 days, i.e. Nirayan Aries Sankranti occurs on 14th April, Baishakh month, spring season. Seasonal Change Decimal Digits 0.53×70.56=37.61 years, Nirayan Aries Sankranti is happening on 14th April for last 37.61 years and will continue to happen for 70.56-37.61=32.95 years.

Example 6: Pushya Paksha Ayanmsha:- 23°3'20.93" or 23.06° decimal, 17 Nov. 2023 AD.

Difference years:- 23.06-23.78=0.73×71.59=52.18 years (+) difference.

Ayanamsh Zero Time:- Ayanamsha is positive, hence it has to be added, 320.22+52.18= 372.40 Ayanamsh Zero Time.

Ganavarsha:- 23.06×25771/360=1650.78 Ganavarsha.

Seasonal Change Days:- 1650.78×365.256363/25771=23.40 Days Seasonal Change. **Refinement Year:-** 23.4/(365.256363/12)/12+0.22 (21 March) = 0.28 years decimal.

Kalisamvat:- 3421.22+1650.78-0.28 Ref. Years=5071.71 Kalisamvat.

Aries Sankranti:- Seasonal Change Decimals 23.40/(365.256363/12)=0.77+2.65=3.41 April,

0.41×30=12.41 days, i.e. Nirayan Aries Sankranti occurs on 13th April, Baishakh month, spring season. Seasonal change Decimal digits 0.40×70.56=27.99 years, on April 13 only for the last 27.99 years. Nirayan Aries Sankranti is happening and will continue to happen for 70.56-27.99=42.57 years.

Example 7: Panchang Diwakar Ayanamsh:- 24°11'18" or 24.19° del, 17 Nov. 2023 AD.

Difference years:- 24.19-23.78=0.40×71.59=28.89 years (-) difference.

Ayanamsh Zero Time:- Ayanamsha is a minus, hence it has to be subtracted, 320.22-28.89= 291.33 Ayanamsh Zero Time.

Ganavarsha:- 24.19×25771/360=1731.67 Ganavarsha.

Seasonal Change Days:- 1731.67×365.256363/25771=24.54 Days Seasonal Change.

Refinement year:- 24.54/(365.256363/12)/12+0.22 (21 March) = 0.29 years decimal.

Kalisamvat:- 3421.22+1731.67-0.29 Ref.years = 5152.60 Kalisamvat.

Aries Sankranti:- Seasonal Change Decimals 24.54/(365.256363/12)=0.81+2.65=3.45 April,

0.45×30=13.54 days, i.e. Nirayan Aries Sankranti occurs on 14th April, Baishakh month, spring season. Seasonal change decimal digits 0.54×70.56=38.33 years, Nirayan Aries Sankranti is happening on 14th April for the last 38.33 years and will continue to happen for 70.56-38.33=32.23 years.

Example 8: AYAN CHALAN SIDDHANT Ayanamsh:- 23°47′05.08″ or 23.78°, 17 Nov. 2023AD.

Difference years:- 23.78-23.78=0.00×71.59=00.00 Parallel of the year.

Ayanamsh Zero Time:- Ayanamsh is a parallel, hence it has to be subtracted, 320.22-00.00= 320.22 Ayanamsh Zero Time.

Ganavarsha:- 23.78×25771/360=1702.66 Ganavarsha.

Seasonal Change Days:- 1702.66×365.256363/25771=24.13 Days Seasonal Change.

Refinement Year:- 24.13/(365.256363/12)/12+0.22 (21 March) = 0.29 years decimal.

Kalisamvat:- 3421.22+1702.66-0.29 Ref. years = 5123.59 Kalisamvat.

Aries Sankranti:- Seasonal change decimal 24.13/(365.256363/12)=0.79+2.65=3.44 April, 0.44×30=13.14 days, i.e. Nirayan Aries Sankranti occurs on 14th April, Baishakh month, spring season. Seasonal change Decimal numbers after 0.13×70.56=9.32 years, Ishtavarsha 2022.88-9.32=2013.56, Nirayan Aries Sankranti is happening on 14th April from 24 July 2014 and 70.56-9.32=61.24 years, 2022.88+61=2084.12. Nirayan Aries Sankranti will continue to occur on 14th April till 12th February 2085.

Ayanamsha and Season Change Difference Table.				
	Ayan.	Season Chg.	Kalisamvat	Aries Skt.
AYAN C.S.	23.78°	24.13d	5123.59	14 April
Lahari	24.19°	24.54d	5152.60	14 April
Difference	00.41°	00.41d	29.01	0 days
Raman	22.75°	23.08d	5049.52	13 April
Difference	-01.04°	-01.05d	-74.07	-1 days
KP (Old)	24.10°	24.45d	5146.16	14 April
Difference	00.31°	00.32d	22.57	0 days
KP (New)	24.10°	24.45d	5146.16	14 April
Difference	00.31°	00.32d	22.57	0 days
Khuller	24.18°	24.53d	5151.89	14 April
Difference	00.39°	00.40d	28.29	0 days
Pushya P.	23.06°	23.39d	5071.71	13 April
Difference	-00.73°	-00.74d	-51.88	-1 days
P. Diwakar	24.19°	24.54d	5152.60	14 April
Difference	00.40°	00.41d	29.01	0 days

The difference between the Ayanamsh of this book and the Ayanamsh of other Ayanamsh writers is the reason for the difference in the time value of the years of Kalisamvat, whereas at present the Ayanamsh writers are showing the nearest years of Kalisamvat in the almanac, but on the basis of their Ayanamsh, the above mentioned Kalisamvat will come.

Baishakhadi month, entered formula:-

Season change month decimal 21 March month decimal/ 12=refinement year decimal, Ishtavarsha Decimal (-) Refinement Year Decimal=Nirayana Ishtavarsha, Nirayana Ishtavarsha Decimal in Decimal Later Digits (×)12= Baishakhadi Month Decimal, In month decimal, digits after decimal (×) (total days of the respective month) = entries.

Hari Om

CHAPTER SEVENTEEN

START OF VIKRAMI SAMVAT YEAR FROM CHAITRA SHUKLA PRATIPADA?

At the beginning of the Nirayan (Vikrami Samvat) years, the first entry of the month of Baishakh also begins when the Sun is at the first point of Aries. At present, Aries Sankranti occurs on 14th April, so the years should also start from that date itself. But the beginning of Vikrami Samvat from Chaitra Shukla Pratipada is **incomprehensible.** If Vikrami Samvat started with the first entry of Baishakh Saur, it will also end with the last entry of Chaitra.

Presently, the years is starting from Chaitra Shukla Pratipada Navsamvatsar Pingal on 9th April 2024 AD, and Nirayan (Vikrami) Samvat is starting from 14th April 2024 AD. Both of them get situated on the first point of Aries on their respective dates. The lord of the day of Chaitra Shuklapaksha Pratipda is the king and the Sun is the minister at the first point posistion of Nirayan Aries. There is a difference of 5 days between the two, this difference is less because there was Adhikmaas in 2023 AD, this difference will increase in 2025 and 2026, Chaitra Shuklapaksha Nav Samvatsar will start in March. So will we change the Vikrami Samvat number in advance by different days...No?

Earlier Vikami and Shaka Samvat were also written to indicate Chaitra Shukla Pratipada. Like 9 April 2024 AD, Chaitra Shukla Pratipada 2080 Vikrami Samvat. Whereas it should be written 9th April 2024, Chaitra Shukla Pratipada 51st Rudra Sangyak Pingal Nava Samvatsar, Chaitra 25 entry 2080 Vikrami Samvat, Chaitra 20 entry 1946 Shaka Samvat. It is worth considering that if the Nirayan year was only 354 days then the need for Adhikamas would have been eliminated. The lunar year is 354.37 days and the sidereal year is 365.256363 days and every third year the deficiency of 10.89 days of Adhikshaya is compensated by Adhikshaya.

The lunar year is a cycle of 60 Samvatsaras, the decision is clearly written in Nirnyasindhu, there are 60 divisions of the lunar year. Samvatsar has special importance in the glorious civilization and culture of India. The new year begins with Pratipada of Chaitra Shukla Paksha. Brahmaji started the creation on Chaitra Shukla Pratipada. Probably, for this reason, it is also considered as a self-siddha auspicious time and the war lord of this day is called the king and the war lord from the beginning of Baishakh solar (Nirayan) month is called the minister. As the seasonal changes continue, the distance between the king and the minister also increases. It meets again at one place after 25771 years.

When Jupiter transits through a zodiac sign at a moderate speed, that period of time is called Samvatsar. Jupiter's average speed per day is 5 degrees. There is a Samvatsara of $30° \times 60 = 1800'/5' = 360$ days. A Samvatsara lasts for one year. In this way, each cycle of 60 years has the name of one Samvatsara, which starts from the beginning of Chaitra Shukla Pratipada and continues till Phalgun Krishna Amavasya.

In daily rituals and other rituals, the name of Samvatsar is taken in resolutions throughout the year. Out of these 60 Samvatsaras, the first 20 Samvatsaras are Brahma Sangyaka, the next 20 Samvatsara are Vishnu Sangyaka and the remaining 20 Samvatsara are Rudra Sangyaka. Which, according to the name, is as fruitful as creation, condition and destruction respectively.

Calculation:- Multiply the current Shaka Samvat by 22 and add 4291, divide this result by 1875 and take the result and discard the remainder. Include the current Shaka Samvat in the profit and divide it by 60, after discarding the profit, multiply the remaining by 60, the obtained product is counted from Prabhav less and becomes the current Samvatsara.

Example-1:- Which Prabhavadhi Samvatsar ran in 15 August 1947, 25 Pravisthe Shravan Shakabdha 1869?
1869×22+4291=45409/1875=24.22, accepted 24, 24+1869=893/60=31.55, sacrificed Labdhi, 0.55×60=33 (Vishnu) to get remainder, got Vikari Samvatsara .

Example-2:- Which Prabhavadhi Samvatsar was running in 14 July 1992 AD, 25 Pravisthe Chaitra Shakabdha 1914?
1914×22+4291=46399/1875=24.75, accepted 24, 24+1914=1938/60=32.30, discarded Labdhi, 0.30×60=18 (Brahma) to get remainder, got Taran Samvatsara .

Example-3:- Which Prabhavadhi Samvatsar was running on 22 December 2023 AD, 1 Pravisthe Paush Shakabdha 1945?
1945×22+4291=47081/1875=25.11, accepted 25, 25+1945=1970/60=32.83, sacrificed Labdhi, 0.83×60=50 (Rudra) to get remainder, obtained Anal Samvatsara.

Example-4:- Which Prabhavadhi Samvatsar was going on on 9th April 2024 AD, 20th entry Chaitra Shakabdha 1946?
1946×22+4291=47103/1875=25.12, accepted 25, 25+1946=1971/60=32.85, gave up Labdhi, got 0.85×60=51 (Rudra) to get the remainder, Pingal Samvatsara.

Chandra Samvatsar Cycle.					
Sl.	Brahma	Sl.	Vishnu	Sl.	Rudra
1	Prabhv	21	Sarvjit	41	Plvang
2	Vibhav	22	Sarvdhari	42	Kilak
3	Shukla	23	Virodhi	43	Somya
4	Pramod	24	Vikriti	44	Sadharan
5	Prajapati	25	Khar	45	Virodhakrit
6	Angira	26	Nandan	46	Paridhavi
7	Srimukha	27	Vijay	47	Pramadi
8	Bhav	28	Jai	48	Anand
9	Yuva	29	Manmtha	49	Rakshasha
10	Dhata	30	Durmukha	50	Anal
11	Ishwar	31	Hemlamba	51	Pingal
12	Bahudhanya	32	Vilamba	52	Kaalyukta
13	Pramathi	33	Vikari	53	Siddhartha
14	Vikram	34	Sharvari	54	Rodra
15	Vrisha	35	Plava	55	Durmati
16	Chitrabhanu	36	Shubahkrit	56	Dundabhi
17	Subhanu	37	Shobhan	57	Rudhirodgari
18	Taran	38	Krodhi	58	Raktaksha
19	Parthiv	39	Visvavasu	59	Krodhan
20	Vyaya	40	Prabhav	60	Kshaya

Note that calculations have been made from Jupiter's moderate motion, not its apparent motion. Therefore, no Samvatsara is missing in the middle.

- Vikrami and Kali Samvat is the Nirayana Samvat, Shaka Samvat is the Sayan Samvat, while in a lunar year there are 360.17 dates, 5.81 dates (360.17-354.37) decay every year.
- So remember! Chandravarsha, Nirayanavarsha and Sayanvarsha are three different subjects.
- Just as when Nirayan Surya is added with Ayanamsh, Sayan Surya is obtained, similarly when Nirayan (Vikami) year is added with seasonal change, Sayan (Shaka) year is obtained.

There are four Navratri:- Navratri occurs at the time nearest to the four main solstice (Ayana+Sampat).

- Basant Navratri from Chaitra Shukla Pratipada to ninth.
- Gupt Navratri occurs from Ashadh Shukla Pratipada to Navami.
- Sharad Navratri occurs from Ashwin Shukla Pratipada to ninth.
- Gupt Navratri occurs from Magh Shukla Pratipada to Navami.

Hari Om

CHAPTER EIGHTEEN

FORGOTTEN

This Ayanamsh is 100% Chitrapakshi Ayanamsh, but it is obtained with exactly 24'18" 23.01'" less values than today's prevalent Ayanamsh or exactly 29 years less, why so? Confirmation of this is possible only when you read the above calculations repeatedly and do the calculations yourself.

The above Ayanamsha etc. calculations have been done from the prevailing average day of Nirayan 365.256363 and Sayan 365.24219 solar year, even if there is a difference in them, the calculation method will remain the same. In the Sankranti calculation, the popular Sayan Sankranti dates have been taken, due to which the beginning of the year will always be from these dates or entries and the end of the year will be at the last point of the previous date. The main reason for giving clarification is to avoid making any distinction.

Time cycle cannot be kept bound, it manifests itself in subtle and long forms. On this basis, calculations have been made from the patterns of Vikrami, Shaka and AD (Grigorian), which are always pure and reliable for Nirayan and Sayan.

Aryabhattaji mentions:- Aryabhattaji mentions in his book Aryabhattiya that "Sixty years of sixty years have passed and three yugapadas have passed. Try more than twenty years have passed since my birth. That is, 60 years. At the time of writing this book, 60 periods (60×60=3600 Kaliyuga) and three Yugapadas (Triyugas) have passed, and 23 years have passed since my birth. On the basis of the above statement made by Acharya, we calculate in which Vikrami, Shaka Samvat or AD he would said this have.

By subtracting 3421 Ayanamsh zero year from 3600, we got 179 i.e. Acharya is mentioned after 179 years from 320.22 Ayanamsh zero year. In the remaining 179 years, if the decimals of 320.22 years of AD that have passed in the Ayanamsha zero year are added, we get 499.22 years, this is the mention of the year 500 AD. If 23 years are subtracted from 499.22, we get 476.22 years i.e. Acharya's birth year is 21 March 477 AD.

By subtracting 78.22 years from 499.22, we got 421, that is, Acharya had indicated this in the first entry of 422 Shaka Samvat Chaitra. If 23 is subtracted from 421 then Acharya's birth year, previous Shaka is 398, current Shaka is 399.

By adding 56.78 years out of 499.22, we got 556. That is, Acharya had given this indication in the first entry of last 556 Vikrami Samvat and current 557 Samvat Baishakh. If 23 is subtracted from 556 then Acharya's last year of birth is 533 Vikrami Samvat and current 534 Samvat is obtained.

By subtracting 3421 years from 3600 years, 179 were obtained, multiplying this remainder by 360 and dividing by Chakra, 2.50° is obtained for 3600 years of Ayanamsha Kali. See the diagram below, explained by picture.

Mentioned year and birth year table.				
		AD	Vikrami	Shaka
1	Kali Years	3600	3600	3600
2	Kaliyug to Ayan zero time	3421	3421	3421
3	Difference	179	179	179
4	Ayanamsha Zero Years	320.22	377.00	242.00
5	Total years (3+4)	499.22	556.00	421.00
6	(-) 23 years	476.22	533.00	398.00
7	Birth Years	21Mar.477	1 Baisakh 534	1 Chaitra 399
8	Ayanamsha (179×360/25771)	2-50°	2-50°	2-50°

Calculation of ayanamsha and season change through the table:- Although the method of calculation of ayanamsha and season change has already been given, here the method of calculating ayanamsha and season change is being given with the help of the table.

Days Period		
Period	Ayanamsh	Season Chg.
1	0.000038	0.000039
2	0.000076	0.000078
3	0.000115	0.000116
4	0.000153	0.000155
5	0.000191	0.000194
6	0.000229	0.000233
7	0.000268	0.000272
8	0.000306	0.000310
9	0.000344	0.000349
10	0.000382	0.000388
20	0.000765	0.000776

Month Period		
Period	Ayanamsh	Season Chg.
1	0.0012	0.0012
2	0.0023	0.0024
3	0.0035	0.0035
4	0.0047	0.0047
5	0.0058	0.0059
6	0.0070	0.0071
7	0.0081	0.0083
8	0.0093	0.0094
9	0.0105	0.0106
10	0.0116	0.0118
11	0.0128	0.0130

Years Period		
Period	Ayanamsh	Season Chg.
1	0.014	0.014
2	0.028	0.028
3	0.042	0.043
4	0.056	0.057
5	0.070	0.071
6	0.084	0.085
7	0.098	0.099
8	0.112	0.113
9	0.126	0.128
10	0.140	0.142
20	0.279	0.283
30	0.419	0.425
40	0.559	0.567
50	0.698	0.709
60	0.838	0.850
70	0.978	0.992
80	1.118	1.134
90	1.257	1.276
100	1.397	1.417

Years Period		
Period	Ayanamsh	Season Chg.
200	2.794	2.835
300	4.191	4.252
400	5.588	5.669
500	6.985	7.087
600	8.382	8.504
700	9.778	9.921
800	11.175	11.339
900	12.572	12.756
1000	13.969	14.173
2000	27.938	28.346
3000	41.908	42.519
4000	55.877	56.693
5000	69.846	70.866
6000	83.815	85.039
7000	97.784	99.212
8000	111.754	113.385
9000	125.723	127.558
10000	139.692	141.732
20000	279.384	283.463
25771	360.000	365.256

Method:- Subtract 321 from the Ishtavarsha and get the Ayanamsha of the remaining years in two separate parts as per the year table. By subtracting 1 and 1 from the Ishta month and date, the Ayanamsh of the remaining Month etc. is obtained in two separate parts as per the respective tables and then adding them, the fraction and decimal Ayanamsh are obtained.

Example:- What will be the Ayanamsh of 22nd December 2023?

2023-321=1702, 11 months, 21 days Ganavarsha received.

Ayanamsha of 1000 years in year table 13.969

Ayanamsha of 700 years in the year table 9.778

Ayanamsha of 2 years in the year table 0.028

Ayanamsha of 11 months in year table 0.0128

20 day ayanamsha in year table 0.000765

<u>Ayanamsha of 1 day in the year table 0.000038</u>

<u>Ayanamsh of 1702 years 11 months 21 days 23.789170</u>

This is very close to 23.79 degrees of the previous Ayanamsha. Similarly, calculate Ayanamsha in future also. If you practice making the year decimal, then Ayanamsha can be calculated easily as per the previous calculation.

Samvat intervening year.

In the previous chapter, the Samvat inter-years were mentioned from the beginning of Kaliyuga till the present, in this regard it was said that the distance between them is decreasing. The same is being shown in the table below. In line one, the interval between the years of Vikrami and Shaka shown in line four is 135.13 varsidas, similarly in line 1 the interval between the years of Vikrami and AD shown in line 4 is 56.91 years, similarly in line 1 the interval between the years of AD and Shaka in line four is Shown is 78.22 years, 78.22 years always remains constant.

The intervening years of line two have been shown in line five in the same manner as above. The intervening years of line three have been shown in line six in the same manner as above.

You see that the seasonal change from the beginning of Kaliyuga to Ayanamsha Shunyavarsha was 0.13 years decimal, hence the difference of 135.13 years is clear. In the zero year of Ayanamsha, seasonal change was also zero, hence there is a difference of 135 years. At present the seasonal change is 0.07 years decimal, hence out of 135 years the interval of Ayanamsha zero has reduced by 0.07 years decimal to 134.93 years decimal. Understand this further also. There is a strong plan to release the said book on Kindle (Amazon), Google Play Book in Hindi and English eBook form in the near future.

Intervening Years Table.				
Era zero-year interval	1	3044.09	3101.00	3179.22
Ayanamsh Zero Years	2	377.00	320.22	242.00
22Dec.2023 Isth.	3	2079.69	2022.97	1944.75
Intervening Years	4	135.13	56.91	78.22
Intervening Years	5	135.00	56.78	78.22
Intervening Years	6	134.93	56.71	78.22

Conclusion:- First of all, you should know that even when the seasons change, the seasons come only on sayan based dates like 21st March, 20th April etc. i.e. the seasons are based on sayan sankranti. Apart from this, Ayan (Uttarayan and Dakshinayan) also occur on sayan based only. The difference of seasonal change falls only on Twelth Nirayan Sankranti and the festivals falling on these Sankranti, like Makar Sankranti, Baisakhi etc.

Hari Om

Dictionary

Ayanamsha=Measurable angular distance between fixed Zodiac and moveable Zodiac.

Ahargana and Vaar=Total Days between Start of yug to Present Date and Day.

Ahar=Days, **Gana**=Calculation of the days

Ayan Chakra=Tropical ¼Moveable½ Cycle

Ansh=Degree

Ayan=Precession

Ayan Chalan=Precession of the Equinoxes

Ayana Gati=Ayanamsha

Nirayana=Sidereal

Bhukt=Spend

Bhogya=Yet to Pass.

Bashant Sanpat=Spring ¼Vernal½ Equinox

Bhachakra=Zodiac

Bhoganshas=Spent Ayanamsha

Cone=Angle

Chakra=Cycle

Char=Diurnal difference

Char Bhachakra= Tropical zodiac

Dainik Gati=Diurnal motion

Dhurv Tara=Polestar

Gati=Pace

Grisham Ritu=Summer Solstice

Ganavarsha= Event Dates(-)321.22 or Event Dates(-)377 or Event Dates(-)242.

Ishtavarsha=Event Dates

Kumbh=Aquarius

Kala=Minute

Madhyam Surya=Mean Sun

Mesh=Aries

Nirayana Sankranti=Sidereal Month

Nirayan Surya=Sidereal Sun

Nakshtra Mass= Sidereal Month

Nakshtra varsh=Sidereal Year

Nirayan Sankranti= Sun enters in one Fixed Zodiac ¼Sidereal½ from Another Fixed Zodiac ¼Sidereal½.

One Ghati=24hrs×2.5

Parikarmana=Revolution

Prithvi,Bhoo=Earth

Pal=1 minute×2.5

Rashi=Zodiac Sign

R.P (Ritu Parivartan)=Season Change

Sayan Sankranti=Tropical Month

Sayan=Tropical

Sankranti=Sun enters in one Zodiac sign from Another Zodiac sign.

Sayan Surya= Tropical Sun

Sampat=Equinox

Sathir Bhachakra, Nirayan Rashi Chakra=Fixed Zodiac, Sidereal Zodiac.

Sayan Chakra=Moveable zodiac

Siddhant=Theory

Sayan Sankranti= Sun enters in one moveable Zodiac ¼Tropical½ from Another moveable Zodiac ¼Tropical½.

Saur Varsh=Tropical Year, Solar Year

Shishir Ritu=Winter Solstice

Sayan Varsh=Tropical Year

Shunya=Zero

Samvat=Era, Year

Shodhana=Refinement

Sthool=Gross

Shunyakaal=Zero time

Sharat Sampat=Autumnal Euqinox

Varsh=Year

Varsadi=Year, Month, Days, Hours, Minute etc.

Vikala=Second

Vipal=1 second×2.5

Author Introduction

Birendra Nautiyal, son of Late Shri Jagdish Prasad Nautiyal, was born on 14 July 1970 in Delhi. Born in a Brahmin family, the writer is originally a resident of village Bastang, PO. Kolakhal, Pauri Garhwal (Uttarakhand). Father, along with working in National Small Industries Building, New Delhi, was an expert in rituals and astrology, mathematics. Therefore, the author's inclination towards rituals and astrology was natural since childhood. The author has voluntarily retired after 23 years of service in the Indo-Tibetan Border Police and has passed the Jyotish Acharya examination with first division after studying the two-year astrological course conducted by the Institute of Astrology at Bharatiya Vidya Bhawan. Naturally, while searching for a Guru, during his service, he found an Astrology Guru in the form of Shri Girish Chandra Joshi Ji in Pithoragarh. On his guidance, mathematical work has been done in the form of supporting writing in his three books namely Ayu Nirnaya Sodha Siddihant aevam Prayog, Kalchak Dasha Se Phalit and Trik Bhav and Chandrama. Now for the first time, the book Ayan Chalan Siddhant, presented in the form of independent research writing, is in your hands.

Hari Om